UNSUNG HEROES

UNSUNG HEROES

A Decade of Writings

Michael Kelly Blanchard

The Attic Studio Press

CLINTON CORNERS, NEW YORK

Published by
THE ATTIC STUDIO PRESS
P.O. Box 75
Clinton Corners, NY 12514
Phone: 914-266-4902
SAN: 298-2838

PRINTED IN THE UNITED STATES OF AMERICA

95 96 97 98 99 00   5 4 3 2 1

Front cover photo: "Roadside Chicory, Meadowland Farm"
Photograph by Trip Sinnott; Colorization by EnterGraphics.

Back cover photo of Michael Kelly Blanchard by David Hawkins.

Library of Congress Cataloging-in-Publication Data
Blanchard, Michael Kelly, 1948–
        Unsung heroes : a decade of writings / Michael Kelly Blanchard.
        p.   cm.
        ISBN 1-883551-10-2 (alk. paper)
        I. Title.
PS3552.L365137U5   1995
814'.54—dc20   95-43135

TO THE
THREE "UNSUNG HEROES"
OF MY LIFE,
my wife
GRETA
and children
ESTHER ANN
and
REUBEN PAUL

*Their quiet love, support, and tolerance
of me has been nothing short of heroic.*

Contents

IV
Woundings

V
Loneliness

VI
Contrition's Harvest

VII
Time Wonders / Now Knowings

Preface

As DIRECTOR OF OPERATIONS FOR Quail Ministries (a tiny Christian arts organization here in the Northeast), I've made it part of my task to lead off its twice yearly newsletter with a writing of some kind. In retrospect, I'm not so sure these verbal meanderings were so much a part of my job description as a cathartic extension for the prose part of my personality.

Whatever their motivation, it's been a delight-filled discipline that I hope to continue in the foreseeable future. At this point, it seems right to gather the best of the batch and put them in one volume. There is no prescribed context or agenda for these musings (though they do perhaps make more sense to the Christian believer). They are my thoughts needing a page to walk on and be seen by the heart's eye.

The song lyrics sprinkled throughout are the best of those that were never recorded in the last ten years. In defining them this way, I'm not "damning with faint praise." They all could have been recorded (in some cases, should have!). Now, at least, they have found a forum where the lyrical portion of their story can be told. For this I am grateful.

While on the subject of gratitude, Joe Dietrich, a friend for many years, deserves a heartfelt nod for coming up with the title, as does Marion, his wife, for her tireless labors as my secretary. I'm also most thankful to Trip Sinnott, my publisher-editor-friend, who so skillfully and lovingly made this fragile dream a reality.

— MICHAEL KELLY BLANCHARD
Christmas 1995

ABOUT THE LYRICS

THE MOST FREQUENTLY asked question of a songwriter is, *"Which comes first, the lyrics or the music?"*

My answer isn't as important here as what's implied in the question. A song is not a song unless both elements are realized. Evaluating a piece on the merits of its tune or verse alone is like assessing a child's personality while knowing only one of his parents.

Many of the lyrics in this book found their original meter and pace as they conformed to an existing melody. Take that sonic grounding away, and they first appear like a dancer without a band, twirling to his own private beat.

When I try to imagine the music (or pulse) with which the lyrics were created, I'm frustrated and can risk passing that on to my impression of the piece. If I allow the words a life of their own without notes or time signatures—disregarding as best I can internal rhymes, for instance—they often walk on their own steam. This is my recommendation for the lyrics contained here.

– MKB

I

A Blessed Bouquet, God's (In)Carnation

Who
He is,
is
why
He
does.

Christmas Letter
("Beginnings and Endings")

At Christmas many Christians remember and give thanks for the point in history when God personally entered this world of "beginnings" and "endings." Before His birth our Lord was certainly involved in our world of time and space, but was never subject to it. He informed His creatures of His loving ways, helped them live by those ways, wept and judged them as they strayed from those ways...but He was still the timeless God, speaking from eternity to a time-bound race. He was the Author of the play and therefore present to some degree in every character, while completely separate from them as well.

He oversaw our births, presided over our lives, and was waiting for us as we died, but He did not have a personal genesis or tale in time, or closing of His particular book.

In a sense, this should be an unworkable concept to His eternal nature. No one ever expected (before Christ) that God Himself would or could be subjected to "beginnings" and "endings." This, to the ancient mind, would have been unthinkable—and is really only tolerable to us because we've lived for so long in the warmth of such unfathomable humility.

But think about it now! Why in the world would anyone free of time and space willingly choose to be confined by it? It's like a free man choosing chains. A bird requesting its wings clipped. A horse agreeing to have its leg broken.

Yet crippled by our flesh and bone and manacled to our clock, Jesus, the only Son of God, came. Like all humans, He sloshed around in that primal sea of His mother's womb. He got a birthday in the usual messy way just like you and I. He had a childhood replete with its share of skinned knees and stubbed toes and, yes, even parental scoldings (remember the temple scene when He was a twelve-year-old?). His teenage and young adult years (though little is known of them) no doubt had their complement of biological "mixed signals" and identity confusions.

He had a mature adult life full of purpose and focus, failures and triumphs, scented richly with friendships and dangerous enemies, joys and sorrows of every kind.

He had a mission of uncompromising clarity and compassion which He saw to its ultimate completion. And, finally, He ended up in some dinky little obituary on page nine, after a brutal murder disguised as "due process," unknown and unloved and even, by many, profoundly hated.

I suspect if the ancients could have conceived of God entering time and space, they never would have imagined such a grim little script for Him to play out. At least for such a sacrifice—such a giving up of rights—we might have greeted Him with the honor due such royalty.

But here the world of old was given a clue to the contrary in the eloquent and heartbreaking voice of Isaiah.

> *He was despised, he shrank from the sight of men, tormented and humbled by suffering; we despised him, we held him of no account, a thing from which men turn away their eyes.*

So rejection and scorn were preordained, predicted of God's visit to earth. Perhaps that wasn't so surprising to the keener observers of this life, as "goodness" has rarely been greeted with open arms throughout our bloody, fickle history.

But still, the inevitability of our resistance to Immanuel (God with us) does not shed any light on why He would choose to come. It only beefs up a compelling case to avoid us. Who would go on a trip to a place where they promised to hang you when you got there?

Who indeed! For it is this ***Who*** that solves all riddles that ask "why." For ***Who*** He is, is why He does.

God entered this world of "beginnings" with all its joy, pain, pleasure, suffering and ultimate "ending" in death because of ***Who*** He is. Jesus did what has never been done before or since. He incarnated life...our life...with love... (i.e. Himself).

He entered our confinements because He is Jesus, the Son of God, the Martyr of Hearts. By His very nature He chose to serve His creation from the "inside out" and honor our flesh and blood with such dignity that the world of humans has never been the same since.

But *who* are *we* that God would choose us as the living vessel He would inhabit? Oh, that's simple (though impossible to understand). We're His beloved... the blessed recipients of Himself. The incarnation is less a puzzle—though no less puzzling—when you see it as a gift of love from the Author to the actor, the "wedding night" between God and humanity, the union of souls with their Savior. And not only did He validate and sanctify us with Himself, He also sent His eternal Holy Spirit to direct our dance in time and space, if we are willing.

After entering our dark windowless cell, He broke open a skylight to His Father's heart that we might see, move and have our being from the perspective of the everlasting. No wonder our hearts never tire of Christmas. When do we ever weary of hearing that God loved us so much He became us, with all our vulnerable "beginnings" and lonely "endings"?

In the light of such **grace** I can only marvel with Isaiah: *Who could have believed what we have heard, and to whom has the power of the Lord been revealed?*

May the awe of that question sing in your heart like a long forgotten carol till it breaks free of your lips in praise and gratitude for all God has done... and continues to do.

Oh, The Love of God
(Barnyard Christmas)

Little Baby in a barn. Deep into sleeping.
You nestle in Your Mama's arms. Dreaming she's beaming.
Oh, the love of God in His tiny Son.
All we thought we had lost has begun in that One.
Little Savior in a shack. Heaven's gone human.
Took a world of woe on His back.
But God knows what He's doing.
Oh, that the love of God might put on our flesh and bones.
So for this world of cold dark nights we might have clothes.
That love had sewn. From head to toe to...heart!

BARNYARD CHRISTMAS

All the animals are kicking in their stalls.
Dancing to a rhythm of a love that's meant for all.
They know without a doubt, and in their way they shout.
A Baby's cried, the gate's flung wide, and man and beast run out.
Donkey and the oxen sing in two-part harmony.

 17

The sheep and goats now join the motley choir.
To the fallen human ear their voices don't agree,
But heaven knows their music is inspired.
Chickens and the ducks join with quacks and clucks.
The sow is singing loud while the rooster interrupts.
The horses neigh and neigh and up there in the hay a
tiny mouse gives out a shout for God on His birthday.
All around the sleepy town there's people waking up.
Wondering where that noise is coming from.
It's late at night, the morning light still has its eyes both shut.
But in the barnyard day has just begun.
So get up off your seats. Join the quacks and squeaks.
Hallelujah, God is come, this ain't no time to sleep.
A serenade of sighs, rises to the skies.
The animals can't hold it back, so why should you and I.

Little Candle in the dark. Glowing, barely showing.
Flame that Father's every spark. Growing, surely growing.
Oh, the love of God to warm our world this way.
To the Stable of our hearts, He's brought us joy, in a
little Boy. Who in our manger did lay . . .
Thank God for Christmas day.

Another Christmas Carol

1. The Redeemer was born in the rumors of morn
   while Gabriel's horn led the band.
   In a midnight rift on the slow shepherd shift
   His star rose and lit up the land.
   Near an old barn of beasts down a dark dead-end street
   in a back-alley suite made of hay.
   God's poor poverty child took a nap for a while
   as mom and dad smiled in the day.
   From the hills around town all the poor folks came down
   and worshiped without a sound in the dark.
   He was not privileged with wealth just a soul like themselves
   who would know how they felt and with love finally melt
   all the fears they had held in their hearts.

2. Oh, a prophecy told of a Child in the cold
   who would come to save souls from themselves.
   He would drive back the night not by power or might but
   inherited light that indwells.
   Now this wonder of Grace would in full measure taste
   all that finite must face in this life.

All the bitter and sweet, all the dreams and defeat,
all the frost and the heat of our strife.
When a man He would serve as God's free walking Word
simply do what He heard living love.
As we stood condemned He would put on our sin
be sacrificed then and in death finally win
back the Garden again with His blood.

3. There were princes who came for they could not explain
the glories unnamed in the sky.
They were driven by truth and the riddle let loose
of a Savior who came here to die.
There were kingdoms they ran with scepters in hand
but they each left their land for the chance
To gaze on the One who from the Father had come
and to bask in the sun of His glance.
With the guide of Star-light they rode day and night
till the babe was in sight and they knew
That all of their days had been spent in a maze
giving honor and praise and the worth of their ways
to fortunes that fade like the dew.

4. Though we run and we hide and fabricate why
and stand by our lies like a bet,
We have long been aware of a dull numbing fear
that our fiction won't clear off the debt.

It takes a baby to show what we're too scared to know
that we long to let go of our pain.
And be free from within and be restored again
and "Abba, Father I'm home" to proclaim.
From the cold cave of doubt with the fire almost out
comes a weak muffled shout through the air.
"Could You really come in and be born in this den
and bring Christmas again to our sad Bethlehem?
Oh, yes, Jesus begin it right here."

Magi

"Have you seen Him?" asked the stranger to a shepherd
by his fire.
"We have long been on our way, sir. We are hopeful but
so very tired.
All the prophets of the ages tell of a holy ruler
born in ruins, who will reign forever.
Have you seen this King, sir?"

"You will find Him in a manger at a back street stable stall.
You will know Him, tiny Savior, by a peace that breaks
down all your walls."
Through the sad streets rode the searchers till they found a
sleeping baby, only child of God and man . . . perfect Lamb.

Oh, they brought Him things that all men treasure,
Gold and frankincense and myrrh.
But somehow they seemed such empty pleasures
when compared to God's own cooing Word.

"All my life I've known the curse of fortune.
Take this gold to know its worthlessness."
"Spirit that gives life to land and ocean.
Take this breath of fragrant frankincense."
"Precious infant, God's infinite ransom.
May this myrrh be worthy of Your death.
No one could be worthy of Your death."

Doubt returning on their homeward journey.
All those months away for what.
A prince of the paddocks. A lord of the lowly.
Just a king for all those who have not.
Then an answer like a fire from a spark.
This One's kingdom is forever in the heart.

Just Like Us

He must've got the message wrong we sent Him 'bout our dread.
We ordered guns and someone strong. Got a baby here instead.
There must be some mistake somewhere, for what good will it do.
When challenged by our foes and fears to answer with a "coo."
The world is not a place for kids, that you and I know plain.
We send 'em back or keep them hid or dress them in our shame.

Oh wait, a prophet's hand is raised. He'd talk now if he could.
He says he spoke in gone-by days, but no one understood.
"The offspring of the Lord," he says, "will come in a disguise,
that our strangest dreams or wildest guess could never recognize."
"He'll come to be, rather then break. Abide rather then rule.
To look for might, would be a mistake. The Prince comes as a fool."

"The very object of our scorn, our ridicule and wrath.
You'll be asleep when He is born, when He dies you'll likely laugh."

"But in this way he'll win your soul and return all your dreams.
For by His wounds you'll be made whole, forgiven and redeemed"
"God is monarch of the heart, He rules from the inside out.
Don't look for him with your smug or smart, but deep inside your doubt."

"From there He reigns over every heartbreak, and understands each pain.
A child will know another child's ache, there's no need to explain."
So yes, perhaps now it does make sense, in melding truth with trust,
that when God made His grand entrance, He was a baby just like us.

Jesus, The Rightful Heir to the Kingdom of Now

IT WAS ONE of those spontaneous, "off-the-cuff" public exchanges that drives political campaign managers to their knees. A young "up-and-comer" was taking on the politically powerful religious establishment in a fiery debate pitting ethnic heritages, against spiritual allegiances.

There had been points well stated on both sides, but as it heated up, the "logical limb" for the young man got thinner and thinner. Prior to this, steadily growing, grass-roots support seemed to follow the man. He had a very engaging, quite human flair, neither wasting nor inflating His words. Many said He "spoke with authority." Now if He just didn't "shoot Himself in the foot," He might be a real contender some day.

And then it happened . . . the young man let slip a whopping anachronism, and they nailed Him on it.

"Your father Abraham was overjoyed," He said, "to see my day; he saw it and was glad."

Gotcha, they thought, and then said, "You are not yet fifty years old. How can you have seen Abraham?"

Then before any of His friends had a chance to say, "No, you see guys, what He really meant to say was . . . ," Jesus spoke the words of a mad man or the very Son of God. *In very truth I tell you, before Abraham was born, I am.*

There, slipping between the cracks of our moments, the eternal heart of God spilled onto our pavement in a clatter of truth that takes the breath away. Saying in no uncertain terms . . . I am neither "was" nor "will be" . . . I am more real than both . . . I am forever NOW.

For years, I took this scene as one of the profound "who" statements of our Lord. The perfect argument for those who suppose Jesus never claimed to be God. Here He names Himself God, as only a Jew would understand, taking the cherished definition of the **Father** (given to Moses) for His own title.

In this one statement He validated and justified all His other claims, forcing the devout Jew to either stone Him or worship Him. It is easy to overlook, however, with such a strong self-proclamation, the startling truth that not only did He declare **who** He was but most emphatically **when** He was.

In stating His "when"-ness as well as His "who"-ness, God gave us a clue to Himself and the release of His power that is like no other. For if you want to get into a building, you not only have to know the **man with the key**, you need to know **when He's around.**

In that one verse, our Lord made it clear that there is no past or future to Him. They are "un-times" that make no sense to His eternal logic of the present. He is not "around" with His "key" in either one of them.

They are words that qualify former present moments and yet-to-be present moments, but are not in themselves valid time terms—for they do not exist as He does in the **now** of NOW! And wherever in time He exists, you will find that His life-changing power dwells with Him as well.

In one brief phrase, He disclosed the only time He can be reached, the only time He inhabits, the only time we can be vessels for His mercy and grace . . . the only **time** to God. You got it . . . *right now!* This can be both comforting and convicting—if we honestly look at our present moments.

The "comfort" is obvious.

Imagine, the very heart of God—Jesus the Messiah—is alive, well and active, through the Holy Spirit, at the pulse of our lives, the cutting edge of our moments. He does not need to arrive on Sunday, or prayer meeting night, or private devotions, or times of tragedy or stress, or times of good fortune, or "religious" moments, to be intimately and powerfully involved with us. He does not need to "arrive" at all for our special moments—He's here already.

What's more, He *is* the moment! He made the moment! He owns the moment! He inhabits the moment! In fact, if anyone needs to "arrive" at the present to meet our Lord, it is us. "Wait a minute," you say, "we're always in the present. How could it be we need to leave someplace to get to where we and God already are?

Enter the "convicting" part to His "when"-ness.

It is true that we wholly inhabit the present with our physical bodies. Big deal! That's no comment on our deep commitment to present living, for, quite frankly, we've got no choice. That's the nature of the physical in time and space. If we had a choice with our bones, I'd lay odds that most of us would be someplace else, because in our hearts (where there is a choice) we often are. Let me explain.

By and large, most of us don't like the present too much. Why? Well for one thing it's too real, too immediate, too either-or, too hard to hide in. We like to have time to think things over...check out our options...take a coffee break and "chew" on it a bit.

But the present doesn't allow that. It says: *now or not now, speak or shut up, do or don't do, commit or ride the fence.* When our physical frames are involved, we have to comply with this harsh regimentation.

But in our hearts, we have the past and the future as well as the present from which to pick when time-shopping. Though neither are "real" like the present is "real," they do exist in a qualified reality because of our imaginations—and therefore often serve as viable alternatives to the brutally frank and frequently unsettling present.

In their best sense, these "trips" to the past and the future can be called reminiscing and dreaming, respectively. Both are holy treasures to be cherished and enjoyed. Both are gifts from God shared only with the crown jewel of His creation...His human children. Both, however (like all of God's wonders), have the capacity to be corrupted. And that,

I contend, happens when they usurp the Rightful Heir of the Kingdom of Now (i.e. Jesus).

And usurp they do! Try this test. Take a moment and honestly evaluate how much of the anxiety, peace, malaise, or joy you feel in the present moment can be attributed to some factor of the past or promise of the future. Confused? Let me share a brief story to help you in this experiment.

A few years ago my sister called with the wonderful and totally unexpected news that my folks had put away some money in bonds for each of their children and that they (the bonds) were coming to maturity in a few weeks.

How nice! How sweet! How much? "Smelling salts, kids, your father needs smelling salts." Suffice to say that to our fragile little budget it was a windfall of "wildest dreams" proportions. We were in debt up to our eyeballs and suddenly with a phone call everything was gonna be all right! Whew!

Surprising to probably no one, a week after the check was received, it was gone. Poof! Not foolishly wasted or materialistically invested. Nope, real practical American reasons like loans and debts and house repairs and medical bills, but nonetheless, it was gone...gone. And that next week I was down...down...which brought to mind how the week before I had been so up...up!

And not just up, but nice...and considerate, too.

What a father I was that week. I played with the kids... read them stories...my time was their time.

What a neighbor I was that week. Why I'd stop to talk about anything, anytime...for my time was their time.

What a husband I was that week...going out of my way to help my wife around the house...cook a surprise meal...anything...anytime, for my time was her time. What a Christian I was that week...faithfully up at dawn for devotions, a heart just brimming with gratitude...spotting God's blessings everywhere in everything...taking time to praise Him and to pray for others...for my time was His time.

One week later, I had no time for anything but the blues. Why? Well I suspect that during that magical week, the part of my "present" that the "future" had held at gunpoint was released. No longer contaminating my "now" with "what ifs," I was free to spend my time on better things. I found my children, my neighbors, my wife and, most importantly, my Lord, waiting for me with open arms in the present moments of that week.

See the point? If most of my present is taken up with an "untime" and all its projected worries, there's precious little space for God to reign where His kingdom exists...NOW!

This, of course, is true of the past as well. Particularly in the areas of old hurts and scares. Ask anyone (which is most of us) who has suffered some form of emotional, psychological or physical dysfunction while growing up if those old wounds don't play a mighty part in how we see ourselves.

This is why the timeless God must bring His ever-present Presence to those past traumas and heal them. He's the only one who can speak to them "presently," bringing all the healing power and compassion of His NOW-heart to our early ashes. When this is done, we are set free to dance un-ashamedly, forever in the "present" of His love.

What, after all, will past or future have to do with us in heaven? Why spend most of our time here participating in and preparing for that which will be non-existent there? NOW is the only clue we have of eternity!

Wait a minute, wait a minute ... This sounds dangerously close to the immediate gratification diatribe of the 60's and 70's. Nope, not if we remember that the difference between living in the Godly NOW and the "me first" NOW is seen in what we do after each moment. The false NOW we enshrine and use as a sacred model for all other moments of spontane-ity... in other words we "past-i-fy" it and thereby maintain an "untime" while claiming to be in the NOW.

The Godly NOW, on the other hand, is often forgotten right after it happens as its remembrance gets in the way of our Lord's new present agenda for us.

No, as I discovered in my "worry-free" week, living in the NOW of God's choosing simply gives us more time to know Him and serve others. The "me-NOW" will always sneak off to the "untimes."

God would have us be free from the pain of the past and the dread of the future—to live and love with Him in the heart of each moment. It's where He reigns and where the seeds of His grace and mercy sprout, blossom, and bear fruit. Remember, the only place our Lord's ministry had little effect was His own hometown where the "past" in His neighbor's hearts would not allow His "present" love to take hold.

"Why, how can He be the Messiah...we know Him... He's the carpenter's son."

Ah, yes indeed, He is that, but not just the One who had his shop in Galilee. He's also the Son of the Carpenter who put His overalls on one morning and went out and made the world!

God in Disguise

At three different post-resurrection appearances, Jesus was initially unrecognizable to His followers. Whether He looked different, or grief-filled eyes blurred their vision, is unclear. That it was part of God's design is indisputable. *God in disguise.* Why?

Well, first it must be stated that this was nothing new. We need not wait till the end of the Gospel narratives to find the Son of God undercover. His entrance into this world, as well as His time walking on it, was more characterized by incognito than trumpets. Let's do a quick review.

Born in a barn where even His first cries were probably drowned out by brayings and bleetings...through a childhood, adolescence and early adulthood, a life so publicly undistinguished that but for a pre-teen encounter with some scholars, there is no historical record of it.

Even the years of His active, visible ministry seemed intentionally shrouded in ignominy. Again and again He frustrated His followers by disappearing just as His fame was about to blossom. Finally, even His torturous death was an un-event by worldly standards, buried in political-religious revelries. The dreams and aspirations of a spirited preacher-prophet fizzling out one spring afternoon on a grizzly cross.

Yep, His life here was mostly "cloak," ending in "dagger." So why, after our final insult to Him was so eternally upended by His glorious resurrection, did He still choose to stay undercover in the days before His ascension?

At least three different possibilities present themselves in the curious, aforementioned God-spottings. Let's take a closer look.

Emmaus

I REMEMBER a close friend reminding me a few years back of our first encounter. The setting was most familiar. A Bible conference center in the Adirondacks. The time was right. The summer of '81. We **were** there. Yet, for the life of me, I could not reconstruct our meeting. This embarrassing (to say nothing of disconcerting) memory lapse was cleared up after he remembered one essential but previously forgotten detail of that week.

"You left early," he said, "after getting a telephone call . . . about them discovering cancer in your father."

Of course, even one of the funniest, most dynamic men I know would be eclipsed by that news coming so unexpectedly as it did, and portending such a dismal future. Personal heartbreak has a way of washing out the details of the present in its terrible tidal wave.

So, emotionally speaking, I can understand how the two disciples on the Emmaus road might have been too "bummed" to recognize the risen Savior. They were, of course, still reeling from His gruesome, ignominious execution.

Jesus, Himself, came up and walked along with them; but something kept them from seeing who it was.

But could there also be a reason He did not want them to recognize Him after He'd defeated Death? I think so.

It's called locating our true self: that "self" which sorrow often frees from our religious posturings and identities. Jesus knew these men did not get it yet. They did not understand who He was . . . or why He was here. He knew to simply arrive as the risen, triumphal Lord in their present state of ignorance would be to court an ugly return of their all-too prevalent tendency of "I-told-you-soing." This, of course, would miss the whole point of His mission and ministry.

No, to get these guys to truly comprehend, He had to talk with them from behind the authentic veil of their despair, despondency and, yes, doubt. Their being religiously congratulatory wouldn't help them understand His words. Their being real would.

This is no less true today. How often have we only understood the deeper truths of God when dressed up in the garments of our grief. So perhaps one reason God disguises Himself is to get at the real us in our pain and heartbreak. On that frequency of truth, we will hear the real Him. He did, after all, define Himself as truth!

"Jesus replied, 'I am the way; I am the **truth**; and I am the life . . .'"

The Man on the Beach

HUMANS HAVE always looked to their toil as a solace for and diversion from grief. So it was with the disciples in the confusing wake of their Master's death. Who could possibly make sense of it all?

On the one hand, there was no doubt about His death. The ghoulishly brutal form of execution known as crucifixion had burned that fact indelibly into their minds. Yet in recent days there had been rumors . . . spottings . . . outrageous tales . . . of the Master's reappearance. Who could sort out such puzzlements? Better to go back to work. To deal with the things you know.

So this spring morning, these professional fishermen were anchored just off shore, doing what they did best in the days before the murdered Messiah. Only now, even this was disappointing. All night dredging the nets and hardly a flapping fin to show for it.

In a brief lull, right after daybreak, they spotted a stranger on shore. It might have been the distance . . . the misty dawn light . . . or the focused tunnel vision the workplace produces. Whatever the reason, they did not recognize the man waving to them from the beach as the same One who had once before intervened with a useful fishing tip.

Again He advised.

"Shoot the nets to the starboard, and you'll make a catch."

Only when a familiar bumper crop bubbled the water did the *déjà vu* of it all occur to one of them.

"It's the Lord!"

Indeed it was! But why here in the common grit of their job? Even later, when He cooked them breakfast and they could see Him clearly, their puzzlement lingered—so much so that no one would publicly acknowledge who He was.

We don't expect God to show up at work. Even the thought of Him there, sleeves rolled up, shoulder-to-shoulder, makes some of us nervous.

His work desk is at church isn't it? Well, at least it is in the religious landscapes we deem proper for a person of His spiritual authority.

Of course, He's Lord of everything, but more the way a CEO is over a large corporation. Not next to you down in the warehouse unpacking crates. Yet here again we uncover our Lord's insatiable hunger for the real (not the religious veneer) in us. If there is some point of our true nature (i.e. true self) that only manifests itself at work, you can bet He'll be there, undercover, redeeming, reshaping, reclaiming and validating that part of our life as well. Remember, the Father's style expressed in His Son, Jesus, is to go to the streets with His love and His healing nature and forgiveness—not wait till the streets come to church.

Nope, His followers obviously had missed the point prior to this moment. So He emphatically hammered it home in the guise of a foreman/short-order cook. We need to remember this as much today as they did then. God does not segregate His presence to *holy* vs. *not-so-holy* places. It's all sacred ground to Him. He's as likely to be found wearing a hard hat as a bishop's miter.

Mary Magdalene at the Tomb

I REMEMBER MY MOTHER recounting that at her sister Elizabeth's funeral, she had been "holding her own" until the graveside service. By this she meant that she had shed all the appropriate tears in private and was being the dutiful care-taker of other people's grief in public.

Somewhere long ago, someone had impressed on her the grievous impropriety of tears in public. She had adhered religiously to this axiom all her life and intended to do so at Betty's funeral. But as Fr. Tom, Betty's favorite priest/cousin prayed the final prayers over the coffin, he caught the grieving stoic off guard.

"Receive into Your eternal rest Oh Lord, Your daughter, Lizzy."

Betty hated the name "Lizzy," Mom told us. Woe unto anyone who would call her that. Anyone, that is, except Fr. Tom. With him, the effect of the name worked just the reverse. It was their special code...his tender term of endearment. No one knew her like he did. Only he had permission to call her Lizzy. Just the thought of that graveside moment never failed to bring tears to my mother's eyes.

So it was at another graveside, ages past, that another woman heard a name that pierced her heart. The brutality of life had so clouded Mary Magdalene's eyes that she mistook the risen Martyr of Hearts for a groundskeeper at the cemetery. In a weary appeal, she pleaded.

"If it is you who removed him, tell me where you have laid him and I will take him away."

Nothing but the intimate language of hearts could penetrate her shroud of sorrow. That special code known only between the two of them.

"Jesus said, 'Mary.'"

The Gardener became... "Rabbuni" (My Master). That special, private, heart-to-heart pipeline between God and His child is the birthright of all believers. His tender way of pulling you out of the crowd. Holding you close and whispering so softly that only you and He can hear.

"I love you, kiddo! I'm mad about you. Always have been... always will be."

In our crazy, frenetic world, these little confessions often come at the oddest times and places, taking any number of forms...

A favorite song on the radio, played just at the moment you needed to hear it. *Thank You.*

A whiff of some fragrance (burning leaves, lilacs, new rain) across a breeze sending the memory mind back to the dearest of moments. *Thank You.*

An act of seemingly random kindness that suggests the style and sensitivity of the Savior. (He often takes His name tag off, you know, when spreading His love.) *Thank You.*

A verse in the Bible read the very moment in your life its meaning and comfort could only fit your situation. *Thank You.*

Did I miss the peculiar way He speaks to you? Then fill in the blank. God in disguise hides around the next moment tucked in our griefs, work and longings, waiting to be discovered in one of the costumes of His creation.

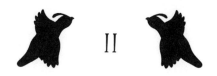

II

Rememberings

*Daddy
come
bring
me
home.*

Glimpses of God

There are glimpses of God in the snow-covered chill
that seeps in the doorways and the windowsills
and blushes the boys as they sled down the hill
to the twirling of girls on the pond scarred and still.

There are glimpses of God in the spring of the earth.
The song of surprise that breaks forth at birth.
The hello of hope that wakes up our worth.
The laughter of love that heals with its mirth.

There are glimpses of God in the summertime plays
that pose like tulips in a backyard parade.
The gossip of crickets as the sun has its way
with the warm and the wind and the dandelion days.

There are glimpses of God in the dying of things.
The autumn of hearts, the fluttering of wings.
The face of farewell in the stares of suffering.
The falling of leaves such a long way from spring.

IT'S ALL WE'LL REMEMBER, AS ANGELS APPLAUD,
THE TRACES OF TENDER, THE GLIMPSES OF GOD.

Bridget
(The Grandmother I Never Met)

Few now remember, the traces have faded.
Some memories are old coats, not thrown out or worn.
Somewhere, it might as well be in the kitchen,
She sat with her knitting just humming a song.
Oh how the melodies spun like a dreidel*
Bouncing and twirling in and out of our dreams.
Each evening the house would turn into a cradle,
She'd rock by the banks of Benimire's stream.

Spring into autumn was mended and passed down.
The hands never stopping no matter how lame.
Winters of mittens replaced in an evening.
Scarves in a rainbow of leftover skeins.
Then when the Yuletide broke open like barrels
and cousins and uncles spilled into the room.
She'd sit after baking and join in the carols
and mimic the men with their stories and tunes.

dreidel is pronounced **dradle**

Bridget, the farther I go in my folly,
you seem to be younger and closer to me.
The rooms full of Christmas, the green hanging holly.
The fiddler is playing, let's join the soirée.
Bridget come dance with me.

Oh, how our seasons are sewn in a pattern,
quilts made of remnants from each of our days.
And Bridget my blanket is full of your moments
Frayed at the edges but warm with your ways.
The gruff sad-eyed doctor said your kind heart was tired
And after you left I believed it was true.
But I think now more likely, it was your desire
to leave for the home of the One who made you.

A Boy in the Back of the Room

In sixth grade Lois was my friend,
    kinda pretty and funny and smart.
She liked me but I didn't know it then,
    love was always ahead of my heart.
We sat in the back by the map display,
    and ran an underground railroad of notes.
She'd read till a dimple would give her away,
    then she'd giggle at what I wrote.
And she'd talk about how things should be,
    and I'd tell her how it feels to me,
And more often then not we'd both agree
    I never knew a girl that way.
She made me feel okay.

At the end of the day by her locker door,
    I'd wait till the coast was clear.
Then getting a charge off the carpeted floor,
    I'd give her a shock on her ear.
"Gotcha!" Then I'd disappear.

One Friday night dance, I picked a slow one,
    and held this friend in my arms.
But with the birth of romance, comes the death of fun.
    I was too young to handle her charms.
See, a twelve-year-old don't know what to do,
    their talk is cheap and quite forced.
It sure feels good that a girl likes you,
    but a corral kind of worries a horse.

So Monday morning she wouldn't look at me,
    'cause I gave her the warning I had to be free.
But by noon all the storming had blown out to sea,
    as I talked her into a truce,
And we both let our ponies loose.

Still sometimes at lunch she'd sit with her friends,
    and I'd catch her looking my way.
And I'd find myself wanting romance again,
    but never knew quite what to say.
Probably wouldn't work, anyway.

In the spring we took our achievement tests.
    Lois always did real fine on them.
I got a score a monkey could get,
    we were never that close again.
She advanced to the college prep
    and I wound up in shop.

She had bright little boyfriends, rings 'round her neck,
    and I made some junk for desktops.

But in that slow track I learned how to write,
    had a teacher or two who turned on the light
While Lois learned how to go out at night
    so I loved her from afar.
As she drove off in somebody's car.

Some years later I spotted a note on my desk,
    it said, "Michael, this is my seat too.
You know, of all of the years,
    I liked sixth grade the best . . .
Your friend, Lois . . . P.S. I miss you."

My friend Lois . . . oh yes . . . miss ya too.

OH LOIS, SOMETIMES MY THOUGHTS SLIP AWAY,
TO A BOY IN THE BACK OF THE ROOM.
WHO SAT NEXT TO YOU WITH HIS TWO FEET OF CLAY,
BUT LEARNED FROM SEPTEMBER TO JUNE,
HOW THE FLOWERS OF FRIENDSHIP CAN BLOOM.

Red Pickup Truck

I was raised on a little farm,
down some road in the heartland.
Big ol' house...silo and a barn,
Ninety acres my Daddy ran.
We were poor, you don't farm to get rich.
Seven kids in a space of ten years.
Common quilt with a lover's stitch,
proud of our laughter, afraid of our tears.

The first four boys had my Daddy's build,
lanky as spruce but not half as wide.
Both of my sisters my Mother's lilt,
small feminine features and practical prides.
Then I arrived on a blizzard morn,
the only baby Dad saw from the start.
Skinny and tall like his four stalks of corn
but restless with reasons and dreams in my heart
like a kitten that wanted to bark.

Daddy saw early I was not like the rest.
"She's a natural," my teacher confirmed.
"With the right kind of training she could stand with
    the best . . .
an actress is born, but she still has to learn."
Part after part he stood in the wings
and watched me as I tilled my soil.
From first grade to high school, I played everything,
as my pot slowly came to a boil.
Out by the wood pond he built me a stage,
in a whispering theater of pines
Where I'd run through emotions from rapture to rage,
and memorize pages and pages of lines.
Just before supper he'd whistle me up.
"Didn't hear a thing," I would lie.
Then out to my rescue in his red pickup truck.
We'd laugh our way home 'neath a sun-sagging sky
to a kitchen of siblings and sighs.

DADDY COME LOOK FOR ME UP BY THE POND,
I'M HERE IN THE PINES JUST AS STILL AS A FAWN.
WAITING TO GIGGLE AND REST IN YOUR ARMS,
AND DRIVE ALL THE WAY BACK THROUGH THE
    TWILIGHT-LIT FARM,
IN YOUR RED PICKUP TRUCK WITH THE ARUUGAH HORN . . .
DADDY COME BRING ME HOME.

My last year of college I married a man,
as true as the blue in his eyes.
He brought me bouquets and accolades with his hand,
and a year later, August, a noisy surprise.
And soon there were two with eyes just as blue,
then a trio of soft little sons.
And just when we thought all the babies were through,
our daughter made four precious ones.

Oh now and again, I think of the times
I performed for the chipmunks and squirrels.
And I sit and I sulk at the way I'm confined
and lament the lost dreams of such a gifted girl.
Then commanding the now, a little actress appears
and her impromptu play cheers me up.
And I suddenly see what I've missed all these years,
is the ride in my Daddy's red pickup truck...
bringing a comfort no life can corrupt.

DADDY COME LOOK FOR ME UP BY THE POND,
I'M HERE IN THE PINES JUST AS STILL AS A FAWN.
WAITING TO GIGGLE AND REST IN YOUR ARMS,
AND DRIVE ALL THE WAY BACK THROUGH THE
*   TWILIGHT-LIT FARM,*
IN YOUR RED PICK-UP TRUCK WITH THE ARUUGAH HORN...
DADDY COME BRING ME HOME.

Iris
(My Little Sparrow)

I see Iris putting my hair in a braid.
No one did it quite like her.
Mom said she asked for me the day she died.
"My little sparrow," she quietly sighed.

I see Iris walking me home after school.
Laughing at the stories I'd tell.
Mom said she honestly called me her friend.
Her "little sparrow" I was to the end.

A LETTER

*"Oh my little girl now that our friend Iris has passed away.
I must finally try and find the words to say.*

Long before I knew the treasure you have come to be.
Alone and so lost, I paid to wash your heart from me.
On that broken day, she blocked my way as I walked in.
The look there in her eyes . . . I started crying.
Then she sang a little song,
all your life long she sang to thee.
"His eyes upon the sparrow and I know he watches me. . .
His eyes upon the sparrow and I know he watches me."

I see Iris watching me from the porch of God.
Waving like she always would do.
Tenderly loving me, telling me still.
"My little sparrow He's watching you . . . and always will."

The Teacher

My grandparents raised me from fifth grade through high school
'cause I was too much for my Mama to bear.
This made me angry and I lived as if my rule was
to find trouble most everywhere.
I smoked in the girl's room, drank well before noon,
and envied the ladies of night.
And swore sooner or later, and sooner'd be better
I'd walk those streets with them all right.
Teachers just passed me 'cause they didn't want to see me
back in their class the next year.
I was branded as "hopeless" and most could care less
but that's when Mrs. Morgan appeared.

In eighth grade I had her, she was known to be quite tough.
A plucky old widow with heart.
But it really didn't matter, 'cause I'd had quite enough
and was planning to take her apart.
I started in early being sassy and surly
with the hope that she'd soon kick me out.

But unlike the rest, she put me next to her desk
and said, "Now you don't have to shout."
She made me eat lunch with her after awhile,
kept me late after school on most days.
I publicly cursed her for cramping my style,
but privately liked it that way,
and would tingle whenever she'd say...

YOU ARE MY DIAMOND IN THE ROUGH.
AND YOUR ROUGH IS WILLFUL AND WILD.
BUT I SEE A SOUL HERE, AS PURE AS FINE GOLD DEAR,
PEEKING OUT FROM AN ANGRY CHILD,
AND THAT JEWEL WILL SHINE AFTER AWHILE.

Little by little a change happened to me,
as I saw just what I could do.
Slowly the riddle of who I was really,
came clearer and clearer to view.
"Girl you got time and such a fine mind"
she'd whisper right close in my ear.
"You're gonna come through, I'm so proud of you,
When you graduate I'm gonna cheer."
For the rest of that year she tutored and trained me
then right into the summertime too.
She loved me with purpose and promise that claimed me
for a life better than I ever knew.

Through four years of high school she watched me uncover
the person she knew I could be.
Though sometimes I'd try foolish things she'd discover
them out and come rescue me.
And I'd often return to where I first learned
I was someone worth caring about.
Wash down her boards, do any old chores,
to be near this dream maker of doubts.
And at graduation I looked for her face
in the crowd but could see it nowhere.
But as I got my diploma I heard her small voice
give out one whoop of a cheer,
and her words came back crystal clear…

YOU ARE MY DIAMOND IN THE ROUGH.
AND YOUR ROUGH IS WILLFUL AND WILD.
BUT I SEE A SOUL HERE, AS PURE AS FINE GOLD DEAR,
PEEKING OUT FROM AN ANGRY CHILD,
AND THAT JEWEL WILL SHINE AFTER AWHILE.

While the Pond Stayed the Same

He would sit in the sun by its shore
(while his eyes would explore).
He would study the lessons it gave.
Now a birth, now a watery grave.
He would stay till the brown bats appeared
Then retreat from his faith to his fears.
He would sail to its distant lands
(with two oars in his hands).
In the morning of make-believe
He would travel the world he conceived
Till one day in the midst of pretend
All the reasons came to an end.

He would skate on its frozen face
(with imagined grace).
He would swim in its silky cold,
Till the summers had been sold.
From its banks he would skim the stones,

like a young man leaving home.
And when he took her to its edge
(like lovers on a ledge).
Their reflections in ripples ran
Waves of woman and of man.
And they'd both laugh back that day
As their children splashed and played.

AND THE POND STAYED THE SAME
THOUGH HIS LIFE SWIRLED WITH CHANGE
BRINGING BLESSING AND BLAME
WHILE THE POND STAYED THE SAME.

INTERLUDE:

Sometimes in a nightmare tremor
he would hear a scream
Out across the foggy shimmer
of some in between.
Someone's dying, someone's leaving,
love has found a fool.
Then he'd wake up gray with grieving
by his childhood pool.

Now he stands in the autumn wind
(dreams end like they begin).
And the days blow round his feet
Where the grass and the lapping meet.

He has wandered from wonder to pain
To come wondering home again.
And the pond as a promise remains
(a hymn's simple refrain).
And he sees in its changeless face
A mere metaphor of grace.
Through all the shivers and shoves
The still water of Fatherlove.

AND THE POND STAYS THE SAME
THOUGH HIS LIFE SWIRLS WITH CHANGE
BRINGING BLESSING AND BLAME
WHILE THE POND STAYS THE SAME.

III

God Gifts

*It's
all
we'll
remember
as angels
applaud…*

Thanks Be to God

"THE GIFTS OF GOD for the people of God," the minister said to his grateful congregation just before Holy Communion.

Suddenly the phrase struck me in a new way. For along with the remembrance of God's atoning sacrifice in the bread and wine, there came to mind many other treasures earmarked for those who choose to be counted among **His** people. (God, of course, would have all people be **His**, but not all people would so align themselves with Him.)

These "treasures" are like so much else of His love, which only make full sense to the active "citizen" of His Kingdom. Priceless pearls like **His Word** (The Bible), elevated from the fine worthy literature it is for the uninitiated student to the timeless inspiration and whisper of hope it is to the believer... or the **peace of prayer** (a true act of faith) that can be such a curious "one way" conversation to the observer and such a life-changing fulfilling communication to the participant... or **Christian community** (the Body of Christ) that dares to put people of greatly divergent differences and sensibilities all in the same "boat" (as it were) with nothing for a common ground save the indwelling presence of their Savior, Jesus. In any other arena, the mere political differences alone would degenerate to "shoot-outs" at the monthly covered dish suppers. But God's gift of Himself to us, His "ornery" people, forces us to learn from, love, and even teach those for whom, in our "flesh," we would hardly have the time of day. Amazing Grace!

There are, of course, many other "in house" gifts, but as I pondered this concept I was made aware of perhaps the most fundamental of them all. It is the "awning" under which all the rest reside.

By letting us know Him personally, He has given us the immeasurable gift of **knowing Whom to thank**! In every situation, He leaves His "card" with His number and address (home *and* office)—not because He needs to be thanked, but rather because we need to thank Him.

Humans intrinsically long to complete the circuit in life's wondrous current of gifts—through gratitude and thanksgiving. It isn't just that we *ought* to say "thank you"... we *need* to. And, what's more, we need to know *to whom* we are saying it!

A personal gift pleads for a personal reply. Even the most out-of-control egotist will privately admit that most of his achievements were co-signed in some way. Regrettably, in this ambivalent age, it's called cosmic fortune, good karma or the "force" being with you—anything as long as it's abstract enough not to be threatening. But "for the people of God" we have a proper name, a royal personage to thank—Jesus, the Father's priceless gift to His aching people. With every "thank you" which our hearts release to Him, He returns the gift tenfold with His presence. So, dear people of God, here is your gift... THANKS BE TO GOD!

Obedience:
The Universal Gift

Have you ever worked at something very hard, spent a lot of time perfecting it, and finally completed it with a deep sense of satisfaction—only to discover someone else did the very same thing more easily in less time and much, much better?

Frustrating, isn't it? All that effort and concentration—just to have somebody else do it with the cavalier detachment of an usher collecting tickets. It's not fair... why do I have to work so hard for what comes so effortlessly to someone else... or, put in another way, why is he/she so much more talented in this than I am?

Well, I don't know why some people are more gifted in certain areas than others... why what is like pulling teeth for one can be done in the sleep of another. But I do know that whatever our gifts are and how much natural skill we have in them, they and their use are not God's key concern with us.

Maturing in our walk as Christians has nothing to do with our native talents or lack thereof save one (and this one everybody has a crack at): **obedience.**

This is a great hope for the many struggling saints who often seem to fall flat on their face in the daily disciplines of their walk, a sobering truth for the few who don't. You see, God is nowhere near as concerned with how well I can do something as with how willing I am to do it whenever and wherever He bids it done.

Our talents are God's gifts to us...no claim or credit can be sent our way; we didn't do anything to earn them. (Our only choice involves what we do with the cultivating of them.) But whatever specific "special" gifts God has endowed to some, He has granted everyone free will. He has given all the honor of the choice to OBEY...and He has indicated through the life, death and return to life of His Son that this willful act of obedience is far more important to Him than any other gift we might own.

I think it's most misleading to see Jesus solely as the supremely gifted Son of God. With this view I will fade spiritually in the great chasm of His gift compared to mine. I'll be tempted to say when seeing the great power of His ministry, "Oh well, that was easy for Him, 'cause He's God."

But when I see Him as the wonderfully obedient Son of God, I can no longer claim He owns a talent beyond my reach. I can no longer use my (seemingly) talentless state as a means of getting off the hook, or as fuel for heavenly directed "potshots."

Simply put, **all** can **obey**, and when we do, even in the (seemingly) smallest of things—a bed made, a sock picked up, a quick word of affirmation, whatever—we come closer to the living heartbeat of Jesus than any acclaim the public display of our gifts might bring us.

The universal gift of **obedience** is the birthright of the reborn. It's the "one-size-fits-all" key to the kingdom of God...and the good news is that every saint owns a copy of that key!

A Fine Thing for Me

I JUST FIGURED OUT a puzzlement. It was the kind you don't know you have, until the moment of its solution. I was doing the laundry. I recommend such "no-brainer" toil when pondering.

Somewhere between the whites and the darks (my uni-colored washing days ended with marriage) it dawned on me why I enjoy the homilies of our assistant pastor so much. With him, one is quickly convinced that what you see is what you get. No frills, no make-up, no religious posturing. Simply a man of the cloth who discovered after forty years of shepherding that the best thing to give a flock is pure, unadulterated you, or is it ewe. (Ouch.)

Ironically, the pun does have a kernel of truth to it. For somehow this retired minister (works for a dollar a year) has not fallen into the temptation (or maybe he's learned from previous falls) of covering up his "sheep-i-ness" with a quasi-spiritual veneer when instructing his people. Because he doesn't hide behind how he ought to appear, or even perhaps would like to appear, the conclusions he arrives at have a ring of authenticity (authority) that sticks to the ribs like good-for-you food.

The listener rarely feels his religious recommendations spring from one to whom such disciplines come easily. His struggle is my struggle. So, his hope in the midst does not feel unattainable to me. He gives himself, fears, flaws, doubts, and all—to a fearfully flawed, doubting congregation. And, you know, it works! As God breaks through for him, we begin to believe He will do it for us. It is a fine thing he gives. For he gives of what he has...merely himself.

I am reminded of another who gave like that. She shows up in all four Gospels, identified as Lazarus' sister Mary in John; implied perhaps as the Mary of Magdalene fame in Luke; and known generically in Mark and Matthew as "the woman" who facilitated our Lord's pre-burial anointing.

Each telling has its unique elements, but Mark's spoke most to me this time around. In his version, Jesus is supping at the house of one Simon the Leper, when this woman arrives. Without a word, she breaks open an alabaster jar of Ointment of Nard and pours it on the Master's head. John recounts that the room fairly exploded in fragrance. This refreshing alternative to the usual gamy fare assaulting Biblical-time noses, was met with surprising hostility by the diners.

The reasons for their bad tempers varied from pseudo-concern for the stewardship of limited funds ("Why this waste? The perfume might have been sold for thirty pounds, and the money given to the poor.") to whispered, bigoted character assaults on the woman and Jesus ("If this fellow were a real prophet, he would know who this woman is who touched him, and what sort of woman she is . . . a sinner").

Then again, perhaps it was nothing more than bald, primal jealousy over a commoner having such easy access to the rabbi. Whatever the cause, their surly displeasure was quickly vocalized. Just as quickly, Jesus came to her defense, saying, "It's a fine thing she has done for me." And a little later on, "She has done what lay in her power."

Those two sentences jumped out at me, for they at once identified and began to answer a long-held question of my heart. It is a question not asked to my religion but to its Author, "What can I do for You? What fine (in Your eyes) thing can I do for You?" Seen metaphorically, the woman's simple actions are wonderfully instructive. Let me offer a brief chronology of her behavior.

First, she located Jesus. Luke says she "learned He was at table . . . " (Imaginary dialogue, "Psst, Mary, Johnny says He's gonna be at Simon's tonight.") Next, she collected that one special thing of hers she could give to Him, an alabaster jar of Ointment of Nard. (Do you hear "The Little Drummer Boy" playing in the background?). Thirdly, resisting all the inner voices regarding the social impropriety of her actions and despite the inevitable public ridicule, she went to where He was and attended Him amidst the raised hackles and ruffled feathers of the dinner guests. In other words, foregoing a more socially comfortable time, she seized the moment. For all this, she was defended—and in fact immortalized—by the Lord of All. ("Wherever the Gospel is proclaimed in the whole world, what she has done will be told in remembrance of her.")

The where, what, and when of my question, "What fine thing can I do for You?" is tenderly illuminated in her brief story.

"Where" for her was wherever Jesus was residing. In a real sense, it is the same with me. Where do I find Him in this week, this day, this hour? I sometimes think He's like Waldo, in the WHERE'S WALDO books. Hidden in a sea of humanity with every possible scene and setting, yet not so much hidden as enmeshed. It helps, of course, to know what He looks like. Waldo's a short, bespectacled dweeb of a guy... but what does Jesus look like to you and me?

Well, He tells us He will peek out from the eyes of the hungry, thirsty, estranged, naked, ill and imprisoned (Matthew 25:35ff). So, judging from present human conditions in this country or any other, there isn't any shortage of "the least of these" housing His contemporary manifestations. He also says that the pure of heart will have the kind of eyes that spot Him (Matthew 5:8). There's another clue. If I fill my heart up with the petty pollutions of this modern society (for me they usually come in through the eyes), I'll have no available vision for the Jesus-spottings that take place daily in every part of my world.

But with all this it is equally important to simply know that He IS there, moment by moment in my day... somewhere. One never doubts, when looking for Waldo, that he isn't right before your eyes; you just haven't spotted him yet and so you keep on looking till you do. So it is with Jesus. If I look hard enough, I WILL find him... every time. Mary "learned" where Jesus was and went there. I must do the same throughout the landscape of my life. I must put my heart's ear to humanity's ground and listen. Heart's ear, not head's. Oh, the head can coordinate and collate the information, but only the heart, the pure heart (or in my case the working-at-being-pure heart) can pick up the authentic rumble of the Martyr of Hearts.

For me there is a variety of places He might pop up. At home certainly, with the kids, shooting hoops or listening to a new "alternative" band or walking the mall. With my wife Greta, listening to her day or spilling my day's guts, or just being with her. Also, at the full-care facility that houses my parents. In the hall-full of faces that plead for a moment of recognition and attention. Perhaps in an unexpected phone call from a hurting friend. In a smile to a flustered waitress expecting my consternation. The list is long and varied. The locations and circumstances are endless and make Waldo's cluttered pages look positively sparse by comparison.

When you think of it, I have a much larger collection of locales to pick from than Mary, and a greater variety of times, as well. The trick for me, of course, is locating where

Jesus is, not where I think He wants me to be. The difference between the two is immense. The first requires little of my ego, ambition, or intellect, while the second skillfully wraps all three in the attractively deceptive package of discerning my spiritual call for the day, week, year...life! No, Mary had it right. Just find out where the dude is and get there.

But what to bring? Mary had a specific element. Ointment of Nard. And its distinct function, pre-burial anointing, to help her decide. How do I know what to bring to wherever I find Jesus? The clue here is not in what she brought, but what was said about it. Remember the line, "She has done what lay in her power"? This constitutes both a relief and a challenge as it applies to me. I am relieved to hear from Jesus' own mouth that doing (as another translation put it) "what I can" is just fine by Him. Nothing fancy or ostentatious, just simply what is in my power to give.

I am relieved, I guess, because for so much of my life, I have measured the worth of my actions by the standards others set—comparing my alabaster jar to theirs and feeling intensely my inadequacy in the difference. Yet, with Mary, even while her accusers tried to trash her choice and its appropriateness, Jesus saw it for what it was and applauded. He would not let comparisons or self-righteous opinion determine the rightness of her gift. It was right for Him because it was in her power to give it. No other standard applied. How liberating to know that whatever you can give is all that's required. I know, I know, Christianity 101. Yet though my head took that course years ago, my heart has never passed it.

Of course, the challenge to giving what lays in my power is that there must be no holding back of whatever it is. It may merely be me, but must be all of that "me." For its worth, if one must judge quantitatively, has more to do with commitment than "street value." Jesus saw all the elements of Mary's gift—the risk, the fear of rejection, the humiliation, as well as the monetary cost—and proclaimed it a "fine thing." He will exercise no less scrutiny with me. I need give Him only what I can, but I mustn't scrimp on whatever that is. David attests in his wonderful 51st Psalm that, in fact, nothing else will do. God doesn't want anything, no matter how costly, that would substitute or detract from my essence. *Thou hast no delight in sacrifice; if I brought Thee an offering, Thou wouldst not accept it. My sacrifice [gift?] O God is a broken spirit, a wounded heart O God, Thou will not despise* (Psalm 51:16,17).

No, the hard side of giving what I can is discovering how unwilling I am, so often, to give it. Not because I can't afford to, or that it's less flashy than someone else's, but because I don't want to and am too stingy to let it go. Usually this manifests itself in the private sector of my world—those jealously held moments of reverie or simple pleasure that get interrupted without any trouble at all by the busy bustle of beings, my sacred agenda upended by what I deem as another's mundane one. Oh, how tedious and unfair. How bothersome.

Oh, how often I would rather pay in tangible shekels what my Lord asks for in service and graciousness.

"Isn't there anyone you can get a ride from..."

"Is that the only time you could get for the doctor's appointment..."

"My, it's been ages...would love to chat but...busy, busy, busy!"

There, mostly in the upheaval of my comfort zone, does the gift begin to approach "fine."

And when might this be? No surprises here. Not when I want or plan or when it's proper or customary, but *now*, when it's right.

How easily Mary could have talked herself out of crashing Simon's party. Everyone but Jesus would have agreed. Everyone but Jesus usually does; which includes the religiously careful, like me. That's why this passage is so instructive to the likes of me. For it is clear in all the Gospel renderings that this woman interrupted a gathering of the religious, which included His disciples. They are the ones having the trouble with this. With very little effort, I can see myself joining them. Such poor timing. No subtlety in the transitions of social protocol. Just show up, stink up the place with perfume, and cry!

God, how clumsy, how bourgeois, how uncool and embarrassing. Will somebody get her out of here before she ruins the whole dinner? Tell her we'll send someone over to see her in the morning. I'll make a note of it...no, I won't forget.

Now, please, get rid of her... excuse me, what were you saying, Rabbi?

"She's done a fine thing for me," declared Jesus. For she gave to Him what she had when she had it. In Luke's account, our Lord's last three words to Mary are, "Go in peace." Ah yes, that's it. Peace that transcends all criticisms from within and without. Peace that cannot be taken away, diluted, or debunked. Peace that lasts a lifetime and beyond, no matter what comes, for it's grounded in eternity. Peace, the gift God gives us for the "fine thing" we give Him. *Shalom.*

Lord of the Lost
(In these Dangling Days)

Here's a toast to the days of our dazzling youth.
The triumph that lies will buy.
Here's a toast to the ways that we've denied the truth
And hid the soul's ache inside.
Everyone's paid too high a price, for a promise
that's turned to pain.
Everyone's watched the fire become ice,
and known in the heart who's to blame.
Then in from the street of Forsaken,
comes the Host long forgotten by all.
And He kneels at the feet of these broken,
to wash off the dust of our fall.

"Captain, oh captain, we're going down!"
Is the cry from the sea of the soul.
The ship is leakin', there are storms all around,
and the crew has lost all control.
Once we were cocky. Once we were proud.
Boasting the brag of our brain.
But our failures and fears fume in these clouds.
Our despair is its bitter rain.
Then there off the bow, through the mist of the mind,
a figure walks up in the spray.
And He calls the heart how a light calls the blind.
"Come to me," is all He will say.

Nobody's sayin' much on death row.
The guilt of our silence is clear.
We've worked every play and trick that we know.
But luck's up and walked out of here.
We've eaten our last meal, made our last call.
Tried one last time to laugh.
Notched our initials on the cold cell wall.
Yeah, this time there's no turning back.

But down at the gallows, seems there's a fuss.
"There's been this mistake," they said.
Then they bring out this fellow, who looks just like us,
and put the noose around His neck instead.

WASHER OF FEET, WALKER OF WAVES.
LORD OF THE LOST IN THESE DANGLING DAYS.
LOVER OF LOSERS WHO HAVE WANDERED AWAY
COME INTO OUR BROKEN HEARTS TODAY
COME INTO THESE RUINS AND STAY.

Trust in the Lord

I WAS PLANNING to write an article on trust. After getting nearly two pages of it down in the computer, something messed up and it went "kapoof"! Zap! Zerp! Blank! I mean, it just disappeared—and I had saved it too!

Now something like that will shake your modern day **trust** right to the core, so perhaps I'm on the right track with this subject. Let's hope so. The text I'd like to use is a familiar one found in Proverbs, third chapter, fifth verse. *Trust in the Lord with all your heart and lean not on your own understanding* (NIV).

Three points seem to be stated here.

    1) In WHOM it is we are to trust.

    2) With WHAT we are to trust.

    3) In what and whom we are NOT to trust.

Trust in the Lord...

THIS FIRST POINT is clear enough on the surface, but often misunderstood or misdirected in living out. Simply put, it is to trust wholly in the Person of God, not in the concept of God; the Person of God, not the theology or culture developed around God; the Person of God, not the people of God.

This, of course, is not to imply that concepts, theologies, cultures and people connected with God can't be trusted much of the time, but simply to state that in our basic soul dependencies, nothing but the genuine article will do.

I have occasionally seen puzzled faces when teaching in retreats. The source of the confusion goes something like this: "I think your songs are great and your ministry helpful, but I don't buy what you're saying right now. What am I supposed to do?" Simple... Rejoice! For you are not trusting in me, but in God as He has revealed Himself to you.

When something I say rings God's bell in you, your spirit leaps to it as John did in his mother's womb to the yet unborn Jesus in Mary. You are trusting God as He spoke through my words to you, for you have cross-checked their authenticity with His Spirit in you, as well as recognized some validation through His Word.

When your spirit is silent, still, or even confused over something I say, you neither betray me nor God by that check. You are simply affirming the fact that trusting in God is larger and more complete than trusting solely in His people. By the way, whenever this happens, don't let it pollute the rest of the talk, be it with me or anyone else. Look over the "broken shells" of words and pick out the "sand dollars" of God to keep.

Of course, implicit in trusting in the Lord is the presumption that one knows personally whom he is trusting. As we all have learned at one time or another, knowing a person is much different from knowing about a person. That is why spouses of famous people will often chuckle at what the world says about their mates.

The press can only speculate on who they are by what they do in public or publish in public records. Their "beloveds"—though they might agree or disagree in part—will quickly add that there is much more here than you can know.

The same is true of a business and its founder. Though a company should generally reflect the basic ethics and principles of its founder, it may take a form that at points has few similarities to his nature.

I remember a few years back when a well-known radio talk show host called our home in response to a song of mine Greta had sent him. We were, of course, quite honored and thrilled, but he said something near the end of our conversation that puzzled me at the time. He said we should disregard the letter we would soon receive from his organization concerning our tape.

This well-crafted "form letter" would state in warm, generic terms that our information was being processed and that we would be notified at a later date about what they intended to do with the tape.

In a gentle, quite vulnerable way, this tender-hearted man of God said to me on the phone, "When you get that letter, remember, that's the organization responding. We have to do that as the volume of letters and tapes is overwhelming. But this call is **me**, responding to **you**!"

So it is with God. One whisper of His in our stilled heart—through His Word as we listen in prayer or through some other means—is worth a thousand lectures or sermons about who He is or what His Church does. The author of Proverbs says that when it comes to the subject of trust, don't fool around on the "outskirts of town" with rumor, speculation and opinion. Go right to the source. Trust the Lord first and foremost and all else will fit or will not be worth worrying about.

...with all your heart...

IT IS INTERESTING to me that the verse does not ask the reader to commit such all-inclusive trust to the mind. This, no doubt, is connected with the last warning *(lean not on your own understanding)* concerning the dubious conclusions one makes when relying on what we perceive to understand; but I think there is a deeper reason as well.

Why do you suppose God picks heart over head here? Maybe because when He requires trust from the heart up, He gets all of us. All of those motives and agendas that rumble around underneath our words and actions. All those things we deny with our mouth (for we don't like being identified with them) but want (and usually get) in our heart.

If God netted our mind alone, He'd get the small fish of our theology, our logic, our rationale, while the "whopper" of our "want to" would still swim free. Only when He commands our heart does He have control of our **will**. The will is the central issue between God and humans, the main spoils over which battles between light and dark are fought.

For years, Greta has heard me grumble in frustration, "Where's their theology?" when hearing yet another married

Christian couple breaking up in the wake of infidelity, or financial calamity, or both. I mistakenly thought that a good solid grounding in biblical principles and ethics, teamed with an active church and vital fellowship with the saints, would "immune" all participants from such behavior. Wrong! All that helps but is no match for a needy, hurt, bitter, rebellious will. For at the core, what *I want* is the only real logic that drives me. Covering that up in "Christianese," God-talk, or theological defenses doesn't change this, it merely hides it from myself and others.

But perhaps a simpler picture is needed here to get at the root. A couple of weeks ago, while on the road, I enjoyed a delightful dinner with some friends after a concert. Following the feast, our waitress brought a dessert menu which included a most astounding selection of pies. (The point should be made from the start that "need" was not the issue here. It rarely is when dealing with desserts.)

I wanted a pie and was having no guilt pangs about it as I perused the list. There were all sorts of wonderful fruit and cream varieties to pick from and I had just about zeroed in on a strawberry rhubarb with a scoop of vanilla ice cream when my eyes picked up the word *pecan* somewhere on the list.

"Oh no, no, no," I thought, "too rich...it's too late at night...there are too many calories!" "PECAN," it screamed from the page. "No, no. I just had a full meal. I certainly don't need it." "PECAN!" Besides, I wouldn't think of having it without a good strong cup of black coffee which would probably keep me up half the night after I got back to the hotel." (I'm afraid, for me, decaffeinated is just not an option in moments like this.) "PECAN!" "No, no, no. Let's be sensible. Your cholesterol's in good shape, last count, but you don't want to go off and do something foolish to tip the balance." "PECAN!" "Okay, okay! Let's just take a look at this here pecan pie and see if there's the slightest case that can be made for it."

At this point, three members of the mind-and-emotions' crack back-up force reported front and center to the chief of staff, General Will. Their subsequent interchange sounded something like this.

"Private Logic reporting for duty, sir."

"Private Theology reporting for duty, sir."

"Sergeant Entitlement reporting for duty, sir."

Looking sternly at these three subordinates, General Will spoke.

"Private Logic, what do you have to say on this matter of the pecan pie?"

"Well sir, it seems to me one key element has been overlooked with all the negative comments on the aforementioned pie."

"And what is that, Private?"

"Nuts, sir. Pecans are nuts! Rich in protein. Good for the body and, I might add, sir, a dandy, all-natural source of fiber. In these fiber-conscious days . . . sir!"

"Thank you! Dismissed!"

"Private Theology, what have you to say on the matter?"

"Certainly nothing new, sir, but I think quite appropriate for this situation."

"Go on!"

"Genesis, sir, chapter one, verse 29, and I quote, *God also said, 'I give you all plants that bear seed everywhere on earth, and every tree bearing fruit which yield seed: they shall be yours for food.'* Pecans fall into the category mentioned in the verse, sir, as they are the fruit, or nut if you wish, of a tree. Based on such information and finding no other verses to the contrary, it is my opinion that God gives the green light on the pie, sir!"

"Thank you, Private! Dismissed!"

"Sergeant Entitlement, do you have anything to add before I make a judgment on this matter?"

"Well of course I do, sir."

"I thought you might. Make it brief. The waitress is due back any second."

"Past records show, sir, that pecan pie has always been a personal favorite since the earliest years, but often denied for a most inadequate reason."

"Which is?"

"Economics! It's often twenty-five to fifty cents more than the other fruit pies, though, on a whole, competitive with the creams and the cheese cakes. This has produced just enough guilt to nix the pie on several occasions. But, as I might remind you, sir, we're being *treated* tonight."

"I know that Sergeant. Any other reasons for the pie before I make a decision?"

"Just one, sir. It's been a long hard tour, with lots of late nights and early mornings and precious few perks along the way, sir."

"Thank you, Sergeant."

"And it isn't like we've been oinking out on pecan pies every night of the week. In fact, I can't remember the last..."

"Thank you, Sergeant!"

"All work and no play makes Jack a dull boy, sir!"

"ENOUGH, Sergeant! DISMISSED!"

"So what are we going to have for dessert tonight?"

"Oh, let me see...why the pecan pie looks pretty good...Yes, I'll have the pecan pie...Thanks."

We can hide it...we can disguise it...we can deny it...with our logical ducks in a row, or our Scripture-quoting, infallible theology, or our life-long list of entitlement experiences that would bring tears to the eyes of the hardest heart...but it still won't change the truth that if we're at the helm of our heart's desire, God is not captain of the ship.

Few people need to know this more than those who openly confess Jesus as Lord. For the temptation to define our agenda as His is great. It is the perpetual task of the believer to daily locate the often camouflaged will and lay it at the foot of the cross. Simply put, when God has our "want to," He has all of us. Giving Him anything less is keeping our foot in the door.

Surely this was never so heartbreakingly seen as in our Lord's agony in the Garden. At His most human and vulnerable, Jesus asked that the cup of our mess-ups and rebellion be passed from Him. Without a second's lapse He added, however, *"yet not My will but Thine."* On the table of obedience to God, the only real playing card is our will.

. . . lean not on your own understanding.

THE SCENE is one of my favorites in cinema. It takes place in a World War II drama, depicted and filmed in Africa. The cantankerous boat captain and the snippy spinster mission-ary have finally realized after a variety of adventures and close calls that they love each other. This revelation, however, is too little too late, it would appear; all their efforts to dodge and maraud the encroaching Nazis have run aground, literally.

For hours, Humphrey Bogart has pushed and pulled his small tug of a boat, the *African Queen,* through a swamp grumpier than his screen persona. As his sole passenger, the ever resilient Katharine Hepburn has cheered from the deck. Their objective is to get to the open sea, which is somewhere (perhaps many miles) from their present position.

What started out slow-going eventually becomes no-going, as the mud finally wins. Bogey gives up, climbs out of the water he's been chest high in, only to discover he's cov-ered with leeches. Boy, what a primal fear chord that scene strikes! In a shudder he confesses to Hepburn, "I hate leeches!" Generations of fans have shivered back, "Me too! Me too!"

The two finally collapse in each other's arms, broken, despairing, exhausted. Too tired to fight anymore, they fall instantly asleep as a gentle rain begins and the camera pans back farther and farther, putting their "hopeless" situation into clearer and clearer perspective. (The eye of God, don't you know!)

It seems from a bird's eye view they're no more than a quarter of a mile from the sea, and by the time they wake up the next morning, the shower has lifted the water table up and they are floating free on the ocean.

This is such a wonderful picture for all those who have given up, hanging their salvation or solution to problems on only those things or people they can understand. There are just too many things in this life that can't be understood within the confines of our limited ability to know.

It seems that older folks tend to understand that truth better than young ones these days. Maybe that's because many of our senior citizens weren't reared on the "hooey" that scientific knowledge is all you need to survive in life. Oh, they learned plenty of facts, but never with the implication that they were enough. Facts were usually tempered with a belief or faith in something or Someone (larger than themselves) which couldn't be proven empirically. They were taught that it's normal, even healthy, to "run your string," come to the end of understanding and submit to a larger Mind. Our modern, out-of-control arrogance has made that simple (and, I feel, preferable) conclusion an impossibility.

A littler farther in Proverbs, the book's inspired writer states, *The first step to wisdom is fear of the Lord, and knowledge of the Holy One is understanding.*

I'm afraid this age is neither wise nor particularly insightful in the larger things—and I might suggest that our failure to observe these basic axioms is a great part of the reason why. We have bought the lie that facts equal truth, as if a square on a page could tell you all you need to know about the nature of a cube.

With that faulty assumption we have conveniently attached (out of context) Jesus' statement, *"the truth shall set you free,"* and whizzo, chango, we have the modern creed, "information equals liberty." We have never known so much and understood so little of what really matters. Our heads are bursting with data, as our hearts are gasping for hope.

I find it tragically ironic that we know, as never before, how humans come to be; yet with that knowledge we yearly choose to extinguish well over a million of our own before they are born. We have leaned on our "own understanding" for decades, and more often than not concluded death is preferable to life. Truly, our Lord's last words to us from the cross sum up our swaggering, head-heavy condition best when all is said and done. *"Father, forgive them, they know not what they do."*

Well, I'd better close before I push a wrong key and send these thoughts into computer oblivion—that twilight zone somewhere between "escape" and "save."

Trust in the Lord with all your heart and lean not on your own understanding.

The Unprecedented Love of God

THE 42ND CHAPTER OF JOB expresses a difficult truth with unsettling simplicity. After all the "ducks" of his logic had been put in a row...his claims to "justified" righteous indignation humbly expressed...his patience with his zealous "friends" establishing a new phrase for tolerance (the patience of Job)...God revealed a glimpse of Himself to Job and nothing was ever the same again.

> *I know that Thou can do all things*
> *and that no purpose is beyond Thee.*
> *But I have spoken of great things*
> *which I have not understood,*
> *things too wonderful for me to know.*
> *I knew of Thee then only by report,*
> *but now I have seen with my own eyes.*
> *Therefore, I melt away;*
> *I repent in dust and ashes.*

"Things too wonderful for me to know"... in a heart-beat silenced his cries of injustice over his recent suffering.

In the light of "one-on-one" with God, all things from his confusions to his conclusions took on a new meaning.

"I knew of Thee then only by report, but now I have seen with my own eyes..." and that made all the difference to how he saw! To wit: the sum of all our information about God does not ultimately add up to God.

With this truth comes some disturbing but ultimately freeing conclusions about our faith. First, we must face the "cold shower" that we can take no comfort in conformity to the rules of our religion or the culture built around it. There are no "group-rates" in Christianity, no "norms" that when followed guarantee success.

You cannot progress vicariously in this faith (in the shadow of another's "walk" perhaps) because **your** walk with Jesus is like no other. You cannot follow the faith by follow-ing someone else's faith, or stake your belief on the spiritual muscle in someone else's arm. Certainly the public disgrace of many highly visible Christian personalities in recent times has hammered home the dangers of "long-distance" Christianity by "proxy." The mistake of looking to humans solely for God's opinions, however, can happen as easily in the local church as it can from the "tube."

Though all those who have gone before or who presently surround us may be a help and an encouragement, ultimately they are no substitute or replacement for the conveyance of God's specific love for us through the intimate, personal affection of our Savior. The "saints" are not God's love, but a partial and flawed example of it. They are an important clue to the treasure, but not the treasure.

We've never known through the humans of our personal history what His love is really like. We have nothing in our experience to which it can be likened. What's more, our concepts of love might be so profoundly different and limited by comparison as to seem His love's very antithesis. The standard ways in which we share, learn, and experience are only partially useful in realizing or describing God's love, for they, at best, only suggest a hint of His full nature, a faint fragrance of His intoxicating aroma.

If, however, God's love has no precedent, it means that all the limited examples of love that we experience in life pale by comparison...in fact can't even be called comparisons! His love is so much larger than any love we know, it doesn't even look like love to us. What's more, it's not based on a partial knowledge of us as all human love is ("If you really knew me you wouldn't love me") but a full knowledge of who we are in our secret-most center. In other words, **His love is so wonderful and grand that there is nothing we could ever do to exclude ourselves from it...except, of course, refuse it!**

Now if that which we think is God's love in our life doesn't feel that "wonderful" or "grand," perhaps that's because the immensity of His affection can never be fully understood as long as we demand to see it through the limits of human love alone. ("I'll know God loves me when He

gives me a husband or a wife . . . or when my mother apolo-
gizes for how she treated me . . . or when I'm appreciated by
my boss or pastor.") How bland a photo of the ocean is to
the real thing . . . no sound or smell or movement or taste! We
need to hear from God Himself through His worship, Word
and whispers, to "taste" in our hearts how deeply He loves
us.

Let me briefly explore these three listening "tools."

WORSHIP

FIRST, we need to hear from Him by thanking and praising
Him. (He inhabits the praises of His people.) I know you
don't always feel all that thankful. You're "ticked" or hurt or
bitter or confused or preoccupied or all of the above or none
of the above. No matter . . . do it. You don't have to know
WHY you're obedient to BE obedient. Sift through the sand
of all your disappointment and anger until you can find
some little "pebble" you are grateful for and thank Him.

WORD

LOGIC has a ring of keys but none of them work on the door
of the heart. Now, as that rusty "door" creaks open, oil it
with His Word. If it's been a while, try Psalms 37, 40 or 51.
Read them not as Scripture to be studied or concepts to be
cognitively entertained, but as a personal message of hope to
a languishing prisoner on his or her own self-imposed death
row. You have been reprieved . . . you are free to go . . . God's
love for you alone has reversed the verdict . . . your broken

heart underneath all that complaint and pity has called the Martyr of Hearts to your cell. The door is flung open wide...He is smiling...it is no trick...Jesus has done what no loved one could ever do for you...He has saved you from yourself—and His Gospel attests to this.

WHISPER

IT IS worth taking note as you bolt out of your "self-cell" through the acquittal of His Word that He will not follow you. Your heart is a prison by your design, but it's a home by His. This home is where He has chosen to dwell, to speak and to grow His will. Slowly, with the artistry and patience of a master, He will turn your former dungeon into a temple. He will do this in whispers that require you to "Be still and know that I am God."

In His whispers, if you are willing to listen, He will set the record straight on who you really are, and what He really thinks of you. There is no compliment in the world to compare to our Lord's most common confession to us..."I love you." Listen for it...**His** voice to **your** ear..."I love you." Not someone else, full of their agendas for your life, telling about His love for you, but Jesus Christ, Himself, tenderly and specifically saying to you in the "home of your heart"... "I love you."

How we need to hear this from God alone, and how afflicted our faith can become with one of two corruptions if our heart is deprived or denied this personal "love song." Either we will convince ourselves (in our hearts) that we are beyond the "limits" of His love...bad, beyond mercy! (A place, I fear, where most of this world lives.) Or as bad, we will convince ourselves that our deeds, talents, or spirituality have earned us the comfort, prosperity, peace and salvation His love supplies! To either aberration I say in the words of Tina Turner, "What's love got to do with it?".

He loves us like no other has loved or will love. So much better and bigger than our human experience, that it's "unprecedented."

The question is not what His love is like, but whether we'll let go of our pre-conceived notions and allow Him to show us the land of His love. A place beyond our limits, laws and fears; the country of His endless heart.

IV

Woundings

The
view
out the
window
is just
a piece
of the
sky.

The Fear of Oz

"It's all the fear of Oz," he said.
"There on the screen of your brain.
The smoke and the fire and that horrible head,
feeding your fear to its flame.
You cower and crawl and promise to serve,
and search the world over in vain
For the trinkets of truth his lies have preserved
or potions that'll postpone the pain.
But when you return from his cruel crusades,
and offer your pride as a prize
You'll finally learn the fool he has made
of you in this false paradise."

Then he ended the class and left the lectern,
as I stared at the stain of his words.
Chilled to the bone by how bitter can burn,
frightened by what I had heard.
And into my life I carried his curse.
Not as a code but a fear.
Dangling a doubt, when death was rehearsed,
that it's all gonna end right here.
Though most of the time I'd pack it away,
choosing belief for my staff,
I could not confine its slow decay
or find much relief from its laugh.

"Excuse me," I said, to the nurse at the desk
as she hid from the hound of my glance.
"The man in Room 5 with the oxygen mask?"
She glared back, "He hasn't a chance."
Disguised in a cancer, and the crumble of years,
it took me a while to connect.
That there lay the theft of my innocent ears
Whose albatross hung 'round my neck.
I prayed for his soul, I prayed for his heart,
and for a flame to believe in my smoke.
My hope didn't hold, my faith fell apart,
but as I got up to leave, he awoke.

His stare was a headstone, a granite gaze.
Wordless with the judgment of death.
Confessing the dark damnation of days
that robs all our boast and our breath.
Then long overdue, I made Heaven's plea.
A rebuttal to his ancient remarks.
Proclaiming to this sad omen of me,
that even the Tin Man found his heart.
And when I had spoken my final appeal,
his arm thrashed the air, then was calm.
The fingers fell open, and slowly revealed,
a crucifix there in the palm.

The Scream

I'M DR. KINCAID, KAREN YOU'RE GOING TO BE FINE.
JUST TRY TO RELAX, I'LL BE DONE IN NO TIME.
THE PROCEDURE IS SIMPLE AND SURGICALLY SAFE
AND WHEN IT'S ALL OVER THERE WON'T BE A TRACE.

Hey Harry you ever have trouble with dreams?
You know, night after night the same one.
Oh yeah, me too, as a kid had a few,
but I thought by now they'd be done.
It's the craziest thing I wouldn't give it a thought,
but I've had it now maybe two weeks.
I'm getting on edge and I'm nervous and tired
and it's starting to give me the creeps.
I know everyone dreams now and again,
they tell me hot food brings it on.
I know after awhile it's bound to improve,
but this one just hasn't gone.
Remember ol' Bill my funny "shrink" friend,
think I'll see if he's free.
There's probably some simple reason for this,
but I just don't know what it could be.

I'M DR. KINCAID, BETTY YOU'RE GOING TO BE FINE.
JUST TRY TO RELAX, WE'LL BE DONE IN NO TIME.
THE PROCEDURE IS SIMPLE AND SURGICALLY SAFE
AND WHEN IT'S ALL OVER THERE WON'T BE A TRACE.

> Well at first it was kind of funny,
> at least for a while that's how it seemed.
> But I tell you Bill now it's old as hell
> this damn recurring dream.
> It's always at my father's farm,
> I'm fishing at the pond
> When from out of the swamp I hear a scream
> that just goes on and on and on.
> It sounds like some baby rabbit
> in some big adder's mouth.
> We heard it now and then as kids
> but never quite this loud.
> I always try to find it
> and it's always just out of view.
> I wake up in the coldest sweat,
> Bill I haven't a clue.

I'M DR. KINCAID, LUCY YOU'RE GOING TO BE FINE.
JUST TRY TO RELAX, WE'LL BE DONE IN NO TIME.
THE PROCEDURE IS SIMPLE AND SURGICALLY SAFE
AND WHEN IT'S ALL OVER THERE WON'T BE A TRACE.

There's not much new to tell you Bill,
I go to bed late and wake at dawn.
That damn dream with its awful scream,
has got me wired like a bomb.
And you know the harder I look the scareder I get.
Like I don't want to know what I'll find.
But the noise just gets louder and louder
till I think I'm losing my mind.
Today at the clinic this girl started to sob...
don't know why, I couldn't go on,
I had to get Harry to finish the job.
Bill what in hell is wrong!

Yes, I'm taking your pills
but they just make me sleep
you don't seem to get what I mean.
Lack of rest ain't the reason
I'm falling apart
You've got to stop that God-awful dream!

I'M DR. KINCAID, JANET YOU'RE GOING TO BE FINE.
JUST TRY TO RELAX, WE'LL BE DONE IN NO TIME.
THE PROCEDURE IS SIMPLE AND SURGICALLY SAFE
AND WHEN IT'S ALL OVER THERE WON'T BE A TRACE.

I know it's real late, you said I could call
God, Bill, I'm really scared.
I finally found out what's making that sound
Oh Lord, you should have been there.

It started just like it always does
at my folks place, there by the pond.
Only this time I swore I wouldn't wake up,
till that infernal cry was gone.
I followed it farther into the swamp
till I came to a blood red stream.
And there on the bank in an old tree trunk
I saw what was making the scream.
It was an adder all right as big as a log,
with his tail thrashing viciously
But Bill it was biting this little child . . .
and the kid just screamed at me!

HELLO DONNA, I'M CALLING FOR DR. KINCAID,
WHO REGRETS HE MUST CANCEL THE APPOINTMENT
YOU MADE.
AS YOU CAN IMAGINE HIS JOB HAS SOME STRESS . . .
SO THE DOCTOR IS TAKING A MUCH NEEDED REST.

Confessions of an Overweight Housewife

We married in the best of times, our secrets still intact.
We stepped across each other's lines and never did look back.
We managed every mystery that a young love can endure.
And in our heart's own history opened many doors.
We went to work, we went to Greece, we went together to the beach,
Our fantasies within our reach, you always held my hand.
Friday nights we'd rendezvous, you'd look for me, I'd look for you,
Talk and talk the whole night through and make our special plans.
Oh now and then I'd see a friend and hate her for her jeans,
that told no lies and spoke of thighs I only had in dreams.
But then you didn't seem to mind, you didn't seem to care.
Our "physical" was doing fine, or so it seemed back there.

Then our children filled my womb, and bruised my body sore.

We didn't want them there too soon, but when it rained

it poured.

A girl for me, a boy for you, their joy melted our fears.

Another one, another two, a full family in ten years.

And through that time, "we" seemed just fine,

I hung the diapers on the line,

You worked two jobs and overtime

It was lean but it was fun.

We took some loans, we built a home, we went in business on

our own,

We had two cars, two telephones, and the work was never done.

But busy phones don't change big bones that ran in my family.

And a new wardrobe ain't what you hold when you're lying next

to me.

You started watching late night shows, I went to sleep instead.

And the intimate that bound our souls, unraveled like old thread.

And now I mourn the death of love, the artifact we've

come to be.

Yet still I long to hold and hug this man who won't touch me.

We laugh and work and guard our pride and talk of when the

kids are grown.

All the trips we'll take to hide the ruins of our home.

Do you recall, early last fall, on a moody Monday we got a call

And though you complained and tried to stall, we drove down to the shore.
A business hunch, then after lunch, we found an old washed up tree trunk,
And watched the sea gulls dive and dunk, just like they did before.
Then to your surprise I dove in the waves.
To my surprise you followed me.
We laughed and kissed like the old days,
the water gave unanimity.

THERE'S A GIRL IN HERE WHO LOVES YOU DEAR,
AND WANTS FOR YOU TO SEE.
THE SOUL UNDRESSED BENEATH THIS FLESH,
THE HEART INSIDE THAT'S ME.
AND IN MY DREAMS I GIVE TO YOU
THE BODY OF MY YOUTH
OH HOW I PRAY THAT SOME DAY
YOU'LL COME TO KNOW THIS TRUTH.

Mimi and Calvin

(BASED ON A TRUE STORY)

Mimi met Calvin at a summer dance,
head over heals right away.
She got her ring as the autumn blanched
and there weren't very much we could say.
Most of the time she was happy enough,
planning the wedding in May.
Though now and again he'd get kind of rough,
she'd laugh and claim that was his way.
All of the bridesmaids wore robin-egg blue,
Mimi a soft pearly white.
All our best wishes went with those two
but wishes don't break up a fight...
though the dishes sure break all right.

They lived in a duplex way across town,
near to his family and friends.
He started right in to knocking her 'round
though we didn't know just how much then.
Billy was born after a year,
then quickly came Donna May.

Mimi said once she got pregnant from fear,
nothing else kept him away.
Shortly thereafter she came to the Lord,
she said, "God alone deserves my fear."
Then one rainy Sunday I too went forward
Calvin laughed, but we didn't care...
peace always came with our prayers.

WHEN WE WERE LITTLE WE'D GO UP IN THE ATTIC,
AND LISTEN TO RECORDS AND PRETEND WE WERE GROWN.
HOW WE WOULD GIGGLE AND RISK THE ROMANTIC
AND TALK TO OUR LOVERS ON MAKE-BELIEVE PHONES.
HER FAVORITE SONG WAS THE LEMON TREE.
SHE'D SING ALONG SO BEAUTIFULLY.
NOW THAT SHE'S GONE IT MEANS SO MUCH TO ME...
OH MIMI.

When Calvin was working he bandaged his bruises
of anger that tore up his heart.
But layoffs come quicker for those with short fuses
and that's when the home came apart.
Mimi would drive the kids out to our folks
for fear of the beating to come.
When it was over he'd cry or just mope around,
begging forgiveness for what he had done.
I couldn't believe she got pregnant again,
she said he was changing, this was a sign.
He fractured her jaw after the birth of their Ben.
"I'm leaving for good," she said,
but I knew she was lying.

For six months at our parents we cried laughed and joked,
sharing the lessons we all had learned.
Then one day after class I discovered a note . . .
Oh Mimi why did you return.

"Sister of my own heart and blood,
please have no fear or no dread . . .
I must return to the man that I love . . . "

Later that night she was dead.
In a coma lay Calvin, by the gun that killed Mimi,
the car radio said quarter past nine.
Then what should come on but the ol' Lemon Tree . . .
"Sister, pray for Calvin's soul, not mine."
I turned that car on a dime.
And as he lay in a room full of sorrow,
I grabbed Calvin's hand and made her request.
"Jesus, this day for there is no tomorrow" . . .
the dying man squeezed back the answer of "yes".

HER FAVORITE SONG WAS THE LEMON TREE
SHE'D SING ALONG SO BEAUTIFULLY.
NOW THAT SHE'S GONE IT MEANS SO MUCH TO ME . . .
GOOD-BYE CALVIN . . . GOOD-BYE MIMI.

Love Has Faces

Right from the start their course they ran, the calendar was king.
They drove their dreams into many lands, wanted for nothing.
Storing up all of their savings from a collection of careers . . .
and sweeping up like shavings the remnants of their fears.
Now and then they'd meet a friend with a carriage in the park.
Both peek in and wonder when their own family would start.
Then right on time . . . they made up their minds
and giggled through the night.
The vote was in, they did begin, and oh, it seemed so right.

At first they took the irony and made it fit the joke.
But waiting grew to a tyranny they wore like a yoke.
And friend after friend the same reply, a precious daughter or son.
Till just a mother walking by would start the tears to run.

So with a list of specialists they sailed the science sea.
Test for test each one knew best but still no baby.
And each month a bigger lump would choke the throat and heart.
The same old dream flushed downstream as the bleeding would start.

LOVE HAS FACES, FORMED THROUGHOUT THE YEARS.
LITTLE TRACES, ETCHED IN EYES AND EARS.
BUT SOMETIMES, LOVERS FIND THE FACES DON'T APPEAR.
THEN TIME REPLACES
THE DREAMS THAT THEY'VE HELD SO NEAR,
WITH FACES THAT RUN WITH TEARS.

(ANOTHER STORY)

I remember the look in daddy's eyes when I broke the news.
If stares could beat you paralyzed, then I'd be black and blue
And Mama with her sorrow all bottled up inside,
said, "We'll talk tomorrow," then left the room and cried.
Later I called Teddy and tried not to sound mad
when a stranger said he'd tell ol' Ted, he's gonna be a dad.

First I kinda loved it, like a secret in my soul.
Thought I'd rise above it, felt quite in control.
Had the same ol' after-hours, the same ol' car of friends.
Till one day in the shower my belly wouldn't tuck in.
Teddy wrote from someplace, said he had his doubts
And in his state it's not too late . . . I threw the letter out.

Now they tell me that this couple are as nice as they can be.
Down to earth real people, not all screwed up like me.
In my heart I feel I should, so the child can be fulfilled.
'Cause what they can't is what I could and what I can't they will.
But sometimes I think about it and water starts to seep.
This child of mine . . . with strangers I'm never gonna meet.

Now I know Jean kept her baby, and I know she thinks I'm wrong.
But I know that I'd go crazy before too very long.
For if this one can find a love, much kinder than my own
I'll take the hurt of giving up to give the gift of home.
And years from now when I look back I hope that I'll be right.
That what I did...you could forgive...I pray with all my might.

I quit my job in August, September 1st I'm due.
I swear it's been the longest month I ever have been through.
Mama said I could move back in...but Daddy's so ashamed,
I try to keep away from him, he won't even speak my name.
I don't drink and I don't smoke and I'm restin' all the time.
And Jean and I took the course at the "Y,"
she says I'll do just fine.
I ain't been sleepin' all that well, so it gives me time to think.
Don't know about heaven or hell, but God knows I'm on the brink.
I feel the baby kick a lot, squirming to get free,
and I think about this child I got and how he seems like me.
After this I'll go someplace and try to start anew,
change my name and hide the pain but I'll never forget you.

AND I WONDER WHAT YOU'LL LOOK LIKE WHEN YOU'RE BORN.
WILL YOU HAVE MY MOTHER'S EYES.
AND I WONDER WHAT YOU'LL BE LIKE FINALLY FORMED,
AS YOU SPEAK IN COOS AND SIGHS.

WILL YOU BE SOME HANDSOME PRINCE ALL IN BLUE,
OR SOME SWEET PRINCESS THAT I NEVER KNEW.
AND I WONDER IF YOU WILL EVER REALLY KNOW
THAT YOUR MAMA LOVES YOU SO...
AND THAT'S WHY SHE LET YOU GO.

(RETURN TO FIRST STORY)

Sometimes some things can't be planned or fit into a form.
For God's the last to play His hand when a baby's born.
Sometimes in the sad of things, a larger joy is found.
One dizzy day the doorbell rings and gratitude abounds.
Photographs on Grandma's lap and everybody smiles.
A house at rest in the happiness of a very special child.
And somewhere down in a different town a mother waves goodbye.
The gift bittersweet is now complete so she breaks down and cries.

LOVE HAS FACES...FORMED THROUGHOUT THE YEARS.
LITTLE TRACES...THAT ARE ETCHED IN EYES AND EARS.
BUT SOMETIMES, A MOTHER FINDS THAT THE FACE
MUST DISAPPEAR.
THEN TIME REPLACES...THE DREAM WITH A PROMISE
SO DEAR.
ONE DAY WE'LL MEET AGAIN...BACK HOME IN
HEAVEN...
SO LOVE UNTIL THEN...GOOD-BYE.

The Last Days of a Daffodil

(FOR LISA)

There was a woman I'm told who was losing a race.
There was peace in her soul, but tears on her face.
She was finally whole, in the heart of an ache.
Having lost all control as she found her faith.
Oh it's the oldest sign on the human wall.
A lover's crime in a victim's scrawl.
Only now this time the betrayed also fall.
By a curse confined to the human hall.

You don't know your life, till you know you must die.
A mother and wife, martyred by lies.
But as she stared at the knife, she opened her eyes.
And Love like a light, exploded inside.
Now mercy is made from the death of our dreams.
Shedding charades, repenting our schemes.
As she let go of her rage, his sorrow was seen.
As she held on to Grace, the wrong was redeemed.

"I'm a flower," she said, "in an early spring field.
Lifting my head, as the Sun is revealed.
Though soon I'll be dead. Death is not as real,
as the garden bed where my seed is concealed."
And blossom she did with a passion to praise.
As terminal hid in a short dance of days.
The gifts she would give will not be replaced.
For the love that she lived had Jesus' face.

The last days of a daffodil are sad but they're sweet.
So giving and fragrant-full, while withered and weak.
A beautiful bugle, sounding retreat.
Dying but hopeful, brave but so brief.
Somewhere in a meadow where time cannot run.
Where now and tomorrow, and yesterday's one
Where suffering and sorrow are banished and done
There are hugs and hellos and a kingdom that's come
for a flower that followed faith into the Son.

There is a Wounding

There is a wounding, deeper than flesh.
Tears bleed from its sad piercing of brokenness.
Years will not mend this. . . or clutter hide.
Shards from both time and space cut from inside.
Some ancient sorrow, so savagely slashed.
Tainting tomorrow, shaming the past.
So old a torment, such familiar pain.
Dull and so dormant, hope forgets its name.

There was a woman, weary from wounds.
Aching and open, weeping in a room.
All of her reasons fell with her tears.
Regrets like seasons wandered through her years.
Bravely forsaking pride she was revealed.
But there in her breaking she began to heal.
Scars for her Savior. Blood for her sin.
Pardoned, she gave her heart back to Him.

Jesus is waiting, patient and still.
While doubt's debating, vying for the will.
All our accusers whisper in the heart.
This place is for losers, so He had best depart.
Then through the window eyes, rippled now with rain,
Looking right past the lies, Jesus sees us plain.
And there's no condemnation for what we've done or been.
Simply one question, "Beloved, may I come in?"

Change of the Guard
(Cut of the Shards)

It wasn't so bad at first
A doctor's appointment or a birthday
No worse.
Then a call to confess the foibles of age.
A joke to digress, quick turn of the page.
Wounds, more or less,
From the war being waged
With the seeping, slow specter of time.

But nothing could stop the hemorrhage of fear
Denial's isolation increased through the years.
Cut off from friends by a steady, slow siege.
Bound to defend the false guilt of disease.
Lethal loose ends tripped my mother's trapeze
And netless she plunged through her mind.

A lifelong romance, its survivor won't save
From a death without dying,
A grief without a grave.
A reluctant divorce that neither one wants
Nursing care forced by dementia's taunts.
A cruel crash course in how the ghost of love haunts
The house two hearts made a home.

Now most of the tender joys of life
Are drained of their blood
Or cut like a knife.
The simplest pleasures have lost their appeal.
Moments are measured by the failure to feel.
Time is tethered to the ruins of real
As Papa is left and alone.

Be sure to convey my warmest regards
To those who downplay the cut of the shards.
But I really must say, I find it quite hard
These days, this change of the guard.

Here in the wings, or is it the stage,
I look on the curse or comfort of age.
Two lives intertwined so long ago
Heart, soul and mind
God only knows.

He gave them some time and a family to grow
But now the job's done
They must wait.

As the crumble of body
The muddle of mind
Tarnish the gold watch at the end of the line.
"All the more reason,"
the priest softly sighed,
"To surrender the seasons and the faith of the eyes.
It's logic's first treason:
To live we must die.
The first laugh they'll share
At the gate."

Hospital Hymn

There are hospital hymns sung in the night,
cutting and clear like a prophet's voice.
Played by sirens and flashing lights,
to terrible tunes that leave no choice.
There are moments that no mind can mold,
with clever cues or changing scenes,
That terrify as they unfold and make a nightmare
out of dreams.

There are words that only God can hear whispered
in the waiting rooms.
Trembling pleas tugged by fears,
carved in the corridors of the marooned.
There are voiceless vows as strong as steel,
that take each other by the hand,
And look through now into the real
where they will understand.

There are days in hours of holding on,
flipped through like pages of old magazines.
Doctor visions; there, then gone,

prescribing promises, denying dreams.
There are faces only strangers find,
hidden in the midnight halls.
Sweeping up the broken time, that's fallen from
a wailing wall.

There are visitors that come to hide
behind their bouquets and get well cards.
Shaping words to fit inside the pockets of their
"best regards."
There are hearts too heavy to conceal.
Longing to take your pain or place.
That love you by the way they feel
and the tears upon their holy face.

Remember once or twice or more,
so young-aware your heart stood still
In some spring-field by Heaven's door,
as winter died to daffodils.

There is Someone beyond boast or brain
who loves you just because He does.
And now "love" will never be the same
what might have been, never was.
For just when men and minds give in
to the lonely logic of despair
This One draws you close to Him and holds you
till Easter is . . . everywhere!

V

Loneliness

Jesus is waiting,
patient and still,
While doubt's debating,
vying for the will.

Loneliness, Part 1:
Disappointment

ONE OF MY earliest childhood memories was having my
tonsils removed at three years of age. Actually, the need for
such an operation stemmed from a lesser known part of the
anatomy called the adenoids, which had swollen up and in so
doing blocked my hearing. (All you "Eye, Ear, Nose and
Throat" people please explain this to the rest of us when
you get a chance). It was my tonsils' unfortunate lot to be
positioned right in front of the offending organs, so when the
word came down that one needed to be removed, both ended
up going.

"You're going to go to sleep for a little while," the gentle-
voiced doctor said, "and when you wake up you'll be able to
hear everything perfectly clearly, just like you used to . . .
though you will have a little sore throat for a while."

Uh-huh! "A little sore" was not exactly the most accurate
way to describe my condition with the return of conscious-

ness. He should have said, "We're going to drag three miles of jagged glass up and down your throat while you sleep."

Only barrels of cold drinks and vats of ice cream could ease my acute discomfort. For this reason I spent a great deal of my hospital recovery time screaming my plight to every passerby who chanced to come within earshot. My song of sorrow no doubt got tiresome to the different shifts of staff members, but for the most part they were quite considerate and accommodating. For the most part.

There was one smoky-voiced, steely-eyed, sergeant of a nurse who wasn't so nice. Whenever she was on the floor, my pitiful cries were matched and bested by her cold, prompt, pointed and effectively grating, "SHUT UP!" This usually reduced my complaints to manageable whimpers. With her, there was no room for argument or explanation, pity or persuasion. I had no options or advocates, simply the responsibility to keep my quivering lips buttoned!

It was an early, tough lesson in one of the harder facts of life. Plainly put, you can't always have what you want or need (didn't Mick Jagger say that once?), and demanding such a thing might be met with open hostility. Though experienced a long time ago, such a "cold shower" of reality left an indelible emotional wound/lesson which I have felt/learned again and again throughout the last 41 years.

There have been many different scenarios or spins on it but always the same basic generic pang. *A need that I expect and assume could and should be met...isn't!* What's more, it's often replaced by the very antithesis of what I desire. Instead of concern for my condition, there's indifference and even at times rejection. Whatever form the dashing of expectation has taken throughout my life (and yours, I bet), the pervading feeling left in its wake is the same...a deep soul-shriveling LONELINESS.

First, let me say that I can offer no solutions to the loneliness born out of dashed hopes and disappointments. For as long as we walk this earth we can expect such things to be a part of our emotional, psychological and spiritual landscape. Humans will always want what they can't have, or need what is not available to them. It is, therefore, inevitable that we will experience the loneliness that such chronic letdowns produce.

Indeed, even those rare few who monetarily "have it all" usually admit that "all" is not enough...or, more to the point, not what they really need. No, I won't suggest for even a moment that such a loneliness is avoidable. It isn't, and believing it is constitutes a dangerous, heart-scarring stroll through the dubious kingdom of denial.

What I *will* do here is briefly discuss how some of the sting from this loneliness might be lessened as we dance our days "down here below."

I was told in school (particularly elementary and middle) that when on the horns of a dilemma, I'd understand much of what presently puzzled me only after growing up. So often was this dodge used in watering down some sticky situation that at times I actually believed there'd be a moment—a specific crossroad in my growth—when the fog would lift. Previously unknown or incomprehensible facts would litter my brain, and lights of understanding would come on all over the place. I'd know beyond a doubt that I had somehow become a grown-up.

Of course, it didn't happen that way. Or at least hasn't yet. Some days (usually bad ones), I hold out the hope it might. But most of the time I'm pretty resigned to the fact that adulthood doesn't arrive as much as it sort of happens— like looking for a certain street only to discover you've been driving on it for the last fifteen minutes. It kind of grows out from under your feet while you're scanning the horizon in search of it. And this is the way it should be. With it comes a weight and a glory that would be too heavy or heady for most of us if arriving all at once—though, to be sure, there are many adult men and women who could tell you the precise moment, usually tragic, when they "grew up." "When my father died," "When my folks divorced," "When my Dad lost his job," "When my Mom went back to work."

What they usually mean is at that moment, through the loss of a loved one or the dismantling of a relationship, their world of carefree, cared-for youth blew up and, for the most part, ended. In these cases, "growing up" is defined more by what has been taken away than by what has been acquired.

But if there could be a point of awareness at which one officially claimed lifelong membership in the grown-up-world club, I'd like to suggest it might be the moment I (or you) realized that no one (not lover, child, parent, employer, etc.) or situation (not home, job, church, etc.) is responsible for my (or your) individual happiness—or, for that matter, capable of truly bringing me (or you) lasting contentment. If we expect this of any person, place or thing, we expect too much and will ultimately be disappointed.

This is a particularly painful pill to swallow in love relationships, as we always like to think we are the sole (or soul) reason for our beloved's well-being. The truth is, nobody could or should take on that kind of responsibility. When they do, it's only a matter of time before one lover collapses in some way under such weight. What's more, with that crumbling comes the added pain and frustration of the other's disappointment and disillusionment.

The ache that cries out from such inevitable ruins makes up the very fabric of human loneliness. Much of our trouble stems from a very fundamental truth we try our hardest to deny. Simply put, *when it comes to my lasting peace of mind and internal tranquility, the proverbial buck stops with me, no one else.*

I know that's kind of a downer axiom, but think about it for a minute. How many times have you curled up in the fetal position of some hurt or betrayal or despair only to realize that the culprit of your funk was more your expectation in the matter than the one(s), place, or situation that let you down.

So often the fierce loneliness that howls in our bones is simply the thinly disguised tantrum of a child who converted his or her unreasonable expectations into foregone conclusions, then blew a gasket when neither hopes nor demands came true.

Yes, yes, yes! Very nice and neat, you say. Very safe! Basically don't dream, hope, long for anything or put your trust in anyone and you'll never have to suffer the disappointment and loneliness and sense of betrayal when the dreams don't come true, the hopes are trashed, and the people let you down. Very shrewd and controlling. Civilized and rational. For you Trekkies, very Spockian! (Are my ears getting pointy?) Sounds like a very head-friendly, heart-empty way to live.

But, of course, that's not what I mean at all. The older I get, the clearer I see the need for life to be more and more heart-friendly...heart-dominated. (Which is not the same thing, by the way, as emotions-dominated. That's another topic altogether.)

No, I believe we need to be more heart-giving in all situations. But what the heart dispenses is not always what it should take in. What or who the heart feeds on for its nutrition, growth and health will more often than not determine how discouraged and lonely its owner will eventually become.

If I have a candy bar for breakfast, the source of my ten o'clock slump isn't all that hard to figure out. I wanted nougat, corn syrup, chocolate, and caramel to do the job of fruit, toast, cereal, and eggs. It can't. Sugar won't fill the shoes of protein and complex carbohydrates.

In the same way, a lover, job, child or a home cannot be expected to satisfy all or even most of our heart's real nutritional needs. Rather than being an exercise in cool, Vulcan-like deduction, carefully screening the sources of hopes and dreams the soul might feed on for its strength is actually the manifestation of a lesson well learned (i.e. *you are what you eat!*).

Nourish the heart with good, everlasting food and you'll have far more energy to lavish and ravish the world with your reckless, abandoned love for it. Far from being careful and cautious, with a healthy heart diet, you'll be known for your crazy, unconditionally dangerous love. No, the heart fed well will live wild and free. The one fed poorly will live imprisoned by chronic complaint and disillusionment.

You might well ask: if people, places and situations aren't the ultimate food for my heart's healthy growth, what's left? The answer to that is both simple and impossibly difficult. For, of course, it's GOD.

The reason GOD as an answer is simple is that He's so available and doesn't require any smarts or gift or breeding to connect with Him. Millions upon millions of humans from all walks and strata of life since He started time have fed their hearts on His food. He has turned no hungry soul away ever—and the good news is He never will. His "supermarket" is open twenty-four hours a day and He's always on site. (And, by the way, His store is in the neighborhood of who you ARE, not who you or someone else thinks you ought to be.)

It's really, as I said, quite simple and yet, as we all know, quite difficult too. Difficult in the same way my taste buds have trouble adjusting to a baked potato or wild rice or broiled fish after scarfing down half a box of Vanilla Wafers. My sweet tooth has been in control—and the better, more useful foods just can't compete with its immediate demands. Every parent knows a pre-dinner sweet snack will pretty much guarantee picky eaters at suppertime. It isn't, of course, that the snack in itself is bad, but rather **when** it's eaten and **how much,** that makes all the difference.

So it is with our heart's primary need for the food of God (which is Himself: "This is my body, broken for you...take, eat"—a relationship with Jesus so intimate that we must ingest His very presence and person to receive its nutrition).

As we entrust our soul's basic nourishment needs first to God—resisting, however imperfectly, the quick-fix sweets of false expectations and hopes—we will find the food of His presence a welcome and ever-strengthening source of real hope through our days, and a valid aid in our life-long battle with loneliness. By the way, it doesn't work to "eat the religion" authored by Jesus as a substitute for Himself. It will become just another sugar sweet to let you down in the mid-morning of your life. It is Himself only that feeds and staves off the hunger pangs of loneliness on our journey.

It should be pointed out as well that God won't take away our loneliness, but He will give us strength to keep it from being overwhelming as we choose to eat more and more at His table. What did the minister say last week just before communion..."Feed on Him in your hearts through faith, with thanksgiving."

It is about this "Him" we are to feed on through faith with thanksgiving that I'd like to conclude my thoughts. Of all the comforts that the Christian faith brings, it seems that none are so perfectly realized as those that go out to the misfit, outcast, disenfranchised (in other words, every one of us at some point). For in the play about our loneliness, God not only wrote the script, He had His Son take the lead part.

If anyone knows what it is to be truly disappointed and let down, it is Jesus. If anyone knows what it is to be truly abandoned and betrayed, it is Jesus. If anyone knows what it is to be truly misunderstood and rejected, it is Jesus. From His first cry as a baby on a winter's night, to His last as the young crucified Messiah on a spring afternoon, He knew as no one else before or since what it is to be lonely. And because of that knowledge, that experience, that cost, and because HE IS LOVE, His wounded hands hold you and me in our brokenness as none other can—not to take away our loneliness, but to entwine it with His, to fashion a rope with our mutual heartbreaks that He will use to tie us to the mast of His heart's boat.

Will the sea be stormy on which that ship floats? You can count on it. Will the waves wash over the bow? Probably. Will the craft at times seem to drift aimlessly without direction or wind in what appears to be a shoreless sea? More than likely. But will the boat ever sink, the rope ever break, the knot ever untie? Never, not ever! For Jesus, the true Captain is at the helm and, having sailed these lonely waters before, He knows, as no one else, the course that will bring us safely into His Father's harbor.

There are rough seas and lonely watches yet to go for you and me, but "Jesus, my crucified Captain" will surely bring us home.

Loneliness, Part 2: Shame

$\mathcal{I}$ had just mowed the lawn. Like cowboys of a hundred years earlier, I headed into town to blow my hard-earned wages on stupid things. In my case, being a twelve-year-old boy in the late 1950's, that meant a blueberry-flavored Popsicle—I don't know whether it tasted anything like blueberries, but that's the color it left your tongue—and a couple of packs of baseball cards.

The dream, of course, was that I might get Roger Maris or Mickey Mantle. The reality was that I'd probably not even get a Yankee, let alone one of New York's reigning home run kings. Reality won out over dreams. After the inevitable letdown, I pedaled back up the long hill from town to our home, under an unusually brutal July sun.

There was a natural spring in a gully off the side of the road that I often visited on such scorchers, and, as usual, I pointed my bike for it. True, there'd be bugs and maybe even a snake or lizard in the tree-covered brook bed, but the water that poured out of a pipe in the side of the hill was worth it. Ice cold. The kind that gives you a headache if you drink it too fast. I collapsed at the foot of the primitive spigot and indulged with abandon.

It was after coming up from my third or fourth guzzle that I noticed it. I'd been too intent on relieving the heat to even casually observe the immediate surrounding of the watering hole. But now, with my belly bulging, I spotted it out of the corner of my eye. It was a magazine. Well, to be more accurate, what I really saw was an image on its cover. It was that of a woman. But, unlike most women I'd seen in my life up to that time, she was different. She had next to nothing on!

Somehow it seems quite fitting that my first totally private encounter with a *Playboy* magazine would be in such a dark, buggy, away-from-the-light-of-day setting. That kind of environment creates the perfect mood for one's relationship to such items. Secretive, hidden, full of shadows. Pregnant with the conflict that forbidden fruit and taboos always have with honest urgings, desires and attractions. It seemed so wrong, yet felt so right. I was all at once free to gaze to my heart's content at what had been previously off limits to my eyes. No one looking over my shoulder to correct or instruct, scold or admonish. Free to simply enjoy. And yet, of course, not really free at all.

For this was the kind of pleasure you could tell no one, share with no one. It bolted shut the door of my soul from the inside out. By its very nature it alienated me from my family and friends, demanding an exclusivity in its relationship. It said with a whisper coy and sultry in my ear, "This is just between you and me. Tell anyone of this and you'll lose everything. They won't understand. They'll be angry. What's more, they'll be ashamed of you."

Yes, yes, that was the key word that described the down side of this unexpected fun...ASHAMED!

There was no denying the attraction to the eyes and other more mysterious senses. No denying the pleasure of seeing what usually was forbidden to my eyes. But these delights had a price and its name was **SHAME**.

Shame by its very nature breeds a special brand of loneliness that is like no other. This is because it almost always sets up a conflict of interest that appears to be impossible to resolve.

On the one hand, you have the thing that caused the shame, which you'd rather not talk about if you had your druthers. Perhaps it's a history of sexual abuse or some physical, emotional or mental limitation or (as with the magazine in my case) something in which you've involved yourself that's enticing but not altogether wholesome or defensible.

On the other hand, not talking about it while not giving it up creates such a vacuum of emptiness and guilt in your heart that you feel detached and self-exiled from those you love and need love from in return.

Shame always creates a struggle between the want of the will and a fear in the heart. Ironically, any long-term solution to this internal battle appears to carry with it what you perceive as lethal consequences. For stitched to the diabolical nature of shame is the half-truth that any lasting cure of its cause or the conflicts and loneliness it creates will probably kill you, or worse, banish the respect and love you have emotionally depended on from your family, church and community.

"If they really knew me," you say in your heart's most private room, "really knew this shameful thing about me... they wouldn't, or maybe couldn't, love me anymore."

The thought of that loss is too great to comprehend, so the shame stays buried and the loneliness it inspires grows in the garden of your heart like weeds in a tear-soaked spring.

Ironically, believers get jostled by an added wave in this turbulent sea of self-deception. For not only does private shame wall off access to their loved ones, it often convinces them that God isn't too accessible either. With God, our flawed, accommodating logic might inspire one of several scenarios.

For instance, if the shame is the type authored by some previous violation or abuse, we are left with the aching question of our Maker's basic care or concern. *How could He allow this to happen?* Over the years, if left unfixed, this sort of doubt/anger/disappointment usually degenerates into a feeling of second class citizenship where God's love is concerned. Printed out on the child-heart screen deep inside it reads something like this: *When I was violated* (if abuse) *or conceived* (if birth defect or physical limitation) *or traumatized* (if some unforeseen calamity befell me) *You* (God) *must have been busy, or out of town, or, even more likely, not all that interested in me and therefore allowed it to happen.*

Of course, there is plenty of razor-sharp theology floating around to refute this intellectually, but that kind of rationale doesn't always play that well in the battered realms of our inner hurts and offenses. We may know in our heads that God loves us despite the discouraging status of our physical, emotional or spiritual state, but someplace deeper than cogent thought, we still may feel left out, misfit, even rejected, and more than likely ashamed by the reality that *what He spared others from was allowed to happen to me.*

It's sort of the opposite of the theological concept of "the elect" (selected by divine will for salvation); it could perhaps be called the theology of "the neglect." However phrased, the atmosphere created in the wake of such perceived abandonment by God is a hothouse for the most soul-poisoning forms of loneliness. After all, there's nothing quite so lonely as believing God exists in a personal way but is too indifferent or apathetic to care about what happens to *me.* That kind of conclusion often breeds atheists. Quite understandably, it's easier to believe there is no God than that the One there is couldn't be bothered with me.

Then, of course, there is the shame bred out of willful behavior that is clearly at odds with the goodness and holiness of God. My magazine encounter and many similar scenarios would apply here.

On the surface, this one seems to be more in the category of avoidable or preventable mortification, but to the believer (or perhaps I should say to some believers), it's not quite that simple.

As I mentioned earlier, the paradox here is that "inappropriate" is wrapped in such attractive, alluring and downright instinctual trappings. Combine this with any number of emotional and psychological deficits from as far back as the womb and you have a primal conflict of interest that can be very hard to shake.

No, I'm not saying it's any less sinful because of this—just loaded with more compelling than decadent reasons for its attraction. What's at issue here, of course, is the shame such fallen behavior produces and the misconceptions about God and his unconditional love that crowd around in its aftermath. Shame's biggest lie where God is concerned is that our shame-filled behavior can at some point so alienate even Him that He'll give up on us, wipe His hands of our sordid little life and say, "I've had enough." That, of course, is what we'd do to some chronic offender of our sensibilities. Cut him just so much slack, then boot him out of the wagon. I mean everything, even mercy, has its limits, right? Wrong! As Isaiah is quick to point out when jotting down the words of God:

> *My ways are not your ways...*
> *my thoughts not your thoughts.*

God's love for us will always be bigger than our lamentable acts of rebellion against it, or our pathetic attempts at self-rule amidst it. Not because I want it to be that way, but because He is that way. If I don't believe that in my heart of hearts, however, my shameful behavior will eventually convince me that He's had enough. With this will come a remorse that only the soul of a believer can feel. Vocalized it would be something akin to, "I had my chance but blew it, and now it's too late!" This is a lie, of course, for lies make up the air of our darkest loneliness. "Too late" is a concept more aligned to our will than God's. Actually, the despair we feel in such moments is bred from self-exile, not God's banishment, and the sooner we own that truth, the sooner we will be able to run back like the prodigal into our Father's forgiving arms.

Let's review. Shame (whatever form it takes) breeds a self-exile from loved ones and God which usually creates an atmosphere of profound loneliness. This loneliness feels impenetrable by such spiritual beams as mercy or forgiveness because its very essence is locked away in a vault that claims to be allergic to the light of truth. It daily proclaims in the heart's most fragile room that if the secret were to be exposed, the whole organism would die or, at the very least, be left in ruins.

Such ruins might take the form of rejection, disinterest, mistrust, or worse, from cherished love ones. So many conclude that living with the loneliness is better than raw exposure and the inevitable emotional abandonment it would inspire. Yes, many live with shame-bred loneliness...and have lived with it for years. But they needn't—for there *is* a way out.

Ironically, the solution (for shame's brand of loneliness has a better shot at being solved than disappointment's type) lies right at the feet of shame's biggest deception...that the cure will be worse than the disease...that exposing the center of remorse will only create a revulsion from a loved one or

God and set up more reasons for shame...that walking through the problem will in the long run be worse and more painful that walking around it.

The truth is that most of what we fear with any certain shame's revelation is more smoke than fire, more illusion than reality. The reason for this is simple. Shame grows best in the dark. Left to shadows and grays and spooky midnights of the soul, it always looks bigger than it is, always preaches a gospel of darkness over light, cover-up over exposure. This, of course, is quite understandable when you realize what happens to it when illumined by the light of truth. It shrivels and shrinks and squeaks like a mouse—though perhaps just moments before it was roaring like a lion from its off-stage shadows.

It's like all fear, really. Remember as a child, or a young adult, or maybe last week when you woke up in the middle of the night and thought you heard or saw something out of the ordinary in the house or in your room? In the midnight half-awake muddle, fear washed over you like an avalanche covering all reasonable explanations in the violence and intimidation of its immediate presence. As you stayed frozen in the dark under the covers, the apprehension intensified, inspired by an adrenaline-fed imagination bent on walking the land of the worst-case scenario.

True, you could've stayed in that terror-stricken state all night long until the light of day chased it away (but what about tomorrow night?), or you could've gotten out of bed like you probably did, turned on the light and faced the music. Well, 999,999 times out of a million, whatever it was that woke you up and set your heart racing wasn't anywhere nearly as bad as you expected. In fact, it was quite easy to understand and manageable to fix. (Perhaps the wind picked up since you went to sleep, and caught an unlatched screen door or shutter.) The power of the thing in your un-illumined state was great, but its size and authority popped like a balloon when you brought it out of the shadows and looked it straight in the eye.

So it is with shame. Keep it in the dark, in the shadows, in the midnight shifts of your life, and it will grow and boss around your inner soul like some bully on the playground. Oh, it may lay low for periods of time, it may even appear like it's no longer a factor (the week the bully got the chicken pox), but that's just part of the dodge, part of the illusionary air it breathes.

Like so many deceptions of darkness, it won't really go away until it's shown up for what it really is. Shame and all the protection we give it hates to be exposed. So there's the clue to curing it. Empty your sad pockets of shame into the lap of a loved one. Entrust your mystery and misery to a heart that loves you. Such a vulnerable, broken act will bring a broom of hope to the cobwebby corners of your heart. The Christian church has a name for such an act . . . confession.

Confession is good for the heart and soul—and, for the most part, will all but eradicate the solitary loneliness shame has created. But even more importantly, it's one of the best ways I know to really understand the forgiving, merciful heart of Jesus.

Someone once said that one of the hardest, most convoluted journeys to take is the foot-and-a-half long trek from the head to the heart. And I believe it's true.

We intellectually believe a lot of things that we intuitively question, doubt or flat out deny. We may cognitively understand that Jesus loves us despite the shame we have caused or that has been left at our doorstep, but if we don't own it (beyond a reasoning way), we probably won't fully enjoy its healing truth.

In my experience, nothing re-educates the fearful heart of the remorse-filled sinner/saint about the true forgiving nature of Jesus like confession. Spouse to spouse, child to parent, parent to child, flock to shepherd, shepherd to flock. Whatever form it takes, it transforms our inner heart's image of Jesus from a folded-arms, tapping-foot, scowling-face, accusatory God to an opened-arms, tearstained-face, beckoning Savior, who always loves us no matter what we did—and always will no matter what we do to break His heart.

Are you lonely from a shame as you read this? Do you deep down feel not even God could forgive what you've done, or release the mortification of past abuse? Bring it to your husband or wife or parent or child or minister, so that they can express the heart of Jesus to you in the matter.

A few years ago, a friend of mine was preaching on confession and its usefulness in the family of God. After the service, an elderly woman pulled him aside and expressed how convicted she was with what he had to say. She indicated there was something she needed to get off her chest. He readily set up an appointment to meet with her the following week.

Just before the planned time of their meeting, she phoned and canceled. He quickly re-booked the meeting but when that time arrived, she at the last moment canceled it as well. This happened again and again until he became convinced she was suffering from an acute case of frigid feet.

Some time later, he spotted this matriarchal parishioner during a weekday at the church and invited her to an impromptu talk on the spot. She was startled and clearly apprehensive, but eventually agreed to join him in his study.

At first, the meeting did not go well at all. She acknowledged that there was something she wanted to confess, but out of fear of his reaction she could not "come clean" and vocalize it.

"You'll think I'm a horrible person and kick me out of church," she cried over and over again, in a profound despair.

None of his assurances that he would do no such thing could assuage her ancient guilt. He was on the verge of "greasing the skids" with the revelation of a past sin or two of his own when she finally blurted out her heinous crime.

"When I was seventeen years old, I stole a deck of cards and never returned them or confessed that I did it. I've asked the Lord many, many times since then to forgive me, but I've never felt forgiven."

With that she dissolved into tears, whispering over and over again "You think I'm a horrible person don't you?"

Actually, all my friend could think about was how glad he was that he hadn't shared with her some of his choice sins.

A deck of cards!

A seventeen-year-old girl left his office walking around in the body of a 73-year-old woman. All because of our Lord's merciful gift of confession.

Didn't Jesus forgive her the first time she confessed to Him? Of course He did. The problem is never God's unwillingness to forgive, but rather our inability to receive His gift. Somehow when her absolution was administered through a human servant on God's behalf, its marvelous healing truth reached her heart as well as her head—and that made all the difference in the world.

If you carry a burden of shame—no matter how big or small (Yes, I know, you may be thinking, "But I've done a lot more than steal a deck of cards!" Hey, so have I.)—take another look at this gift called confession and see if it might be time in your journey to leave the loneliness of shame behind.

If Lydia Were Here

If Lydia were here, she'd welcome you in,
with the shy kindly grin of her father.
The coarse auburn hair her grandmother spun
would be tied in a bun like her mother.
Her voice salty clear would hint of a laugh,
but hold it all back like a sentinel.
Her eyes round and rare, would quick steal the scene,
two softly sad green little emeralds.
Dressed in the armor of summer vacation,
halter and cut-offs and swimming pool thongs.
Brown with the blemish of the sun's education,
she'd charm you with beauty and before very long,
you'd feel right at home, like you always had known her.

If Lydia were here, her brothers would shame
and reveal the name of her new beau.
With a half angry stare, while blushing with pride,
she'd vaguely deny it was so.
Though they would jeer, they'd love her with need
and come when they'd bleed for her caring.

The sister upstairs, who'd help them with their math
and calm Daddy's wrath, when raging.
Famed for her salads and blueberry pancakes,
she'd whittle her father with varied cuisines.
Known for her neighborhood collection of heartaches.
The princess that princes want for their queen.
Want for their wife, for the rest of their life.

INTERLUDE
We were so in love that summer,
lingering with every kiss.
Washing each embrace with wonder,
longing that our love might live like this.
So of course she appeared,
passion pleads with its tears,
make this moment we shared last forever, last forever,
forever, forever, for Lydia.

But Lydia's not here, she left years ago,
before we could know her sweet love song.
Trapped by our fear of too much too soon,
one gray afternoon she was gone.
Lydia, my dear, I want you to know,
though I let you go I'm so sorry.
All the children I've reared have been boys since you left.
You were the only girl guest of this body.
Though I was groggy and numb to emotion,
a trace of devotion, ever so weak.

Heard the nurse with the red hair,
as she left with the white pail say,
"The fetus was female ... about thirteen weeks"
Good-bye my daughter forgive me and your father.
If Lydia were here I feel she'd forgive,
how else could I live with this burden.
God knows the tears I've shed since that day,
and He's stored them away ... for our reunion.

Loneliness, Part 3:
Aloneness
(Finding the "Just 'Cuz" Love of God)

SHE HOPPED OUT OF HER CAR to fetch a morning paper as I jogged by. Blaring from the radio was the mindless patter of a co-ed "morning team." Even in the time it took me to run by, I heard enough to wonder all the way home why anyone at any time of day would willingly subject themselves to such annoying and affronting drivel.

It came to me in the shower. Of course! She's stuck in her car alone and she doesn't like it. Most of us don't. We'll endure even the cascading, vacuous verbiage of talk radio over the unsettling "sound of silence."

There are lots of reasons for this, of course, most of which would take too long to deal with here. One pretty safe, generic explanation, though, might be that "alone times" tend to collect our personal doubts and apprehensions and drape them on our thoughts like cheap, ill-fitting furniture covers. It's no fun and not very constructive, so we opt for noise over neurosis. But it doesn't have to be like that. Being alone or doing things alone without help from others can be a good thing, a nurturing thing, and for the believer, a most necessary thing. Let me show you what I mean.

Every parent knows when the moment comes. For years you let your child win at the game, whatever it is. They might sense you threw it, but winning was more important at that point than reality. Then one day it changes. "Did you let me win, Dad?" From then on, it's a slippery descent into the world of benign parental deceit until one proud day you breathlessly wheeze back, "No (gasp) . . . you beat me (cough) . . . fair and square."

The grin that covers the face of the victorious challenger is not just conqueror's countenance but healthy self-esteem as well. It is the manifestation of an important personal awareness and validation that cannot be gotten with a group and/or phony win.

"I did it! I actually beat Dad!" It's the distinct fruit of achieving something alone. As much as we all find comfort and security in a crowd, few will deny the personal satisfaction of a solo flight done well. No mystery here, for in one fell swoop we've pulled off what a thousand group conquests couldn't. We've learned that we are capable and sufficient in whatever discipline without the immediate help of others. If we don't let it go to our heads, it can be a very useful part of our character development.

In God's language, "character development" is just another word for personal, growing faith. And up to a certain point, the unique value of solitary accomplishments applies here as well.

Throughout the history of His way with humans, God has demonstrated again and again His propensity for going one-on-one with us. That's why He has no grandchildren, only children. He wants our connecting with Him to start, grow and remain as intimate as a parent-child relationship, like the one Jesus demonstrated He had with His Father throughout His life.

He's not opposed to the gathering of His family, of course. But the cornerstone of His love is realized in a very intimate and individual way. No amount of "group-rates" religion can take the place of the personal confession of His affection for you and me in the special, unique way He chooses to reveal Himself to you and me... "I love you," whispered in the heart's ear. It is the building block of our faith and personal esteem as a child of God.

But here's where the metaphor of "whoopin' Dad all by myself" doesn't work. For the approval we receive from God's renegade, reckless, personal love is not based on anything we've done or won or accomplished alone or otherwise. His affection for us is not so much the validation of our inherent lovableness or usefulness as it is the expression of His nature to love us... "just 'cuz." As St. Paul has attested from Romans to Ephesians and beyond, God quite bluntly doesn't love you or me for anything we've ever done. It's a left hook to our obsessive, doing egos.

But look at it this way, the converse of that statement is equally true. He won't stop loving you or me even if we stop being lovable or useful. He loves us "just 'cuz" and that's just the way it is.

Ironically, "just 'cuz" love is received best on the lonely watches, in the lonely places. It gets all muddled and confused in the funky, finicky world of human approval ratings and opinion polls. Jesus knew this well. He no sooner fed the five thousand when He went looking for a lonely place to be with his Dad . . . alone. He knew what the likes of you or me or Peter would say in the wake of His wonders. How fickle, dangerous and false our star-struck affections were. And when we spewed out our palaver, He called us Satan and told us to get behind Him. He knew that only His Father's voice was truly truth and it was best heard "far from the madding crowd."

So aloneness might not be so bad after all. Especially if it is the place we can hear God's love-call best. Seen in that light, it's downright essential, like food or drink. To quote our Lord, this is "real food" and "real drink."

Beloved of God, go find some lonely place and be alone with the One who loves you "just 'cuz."

VI

Contrition's Harvest

*Lover
of
losers
who
have
wandered
away...*

Of Carrots, Cars, and Grace

IN THE SEVENTH CHAPTER of Luke's Gospel, there is a scene described that has rarely failed to bring tears to my eyes. In a funny way, it both frightens and comforts me—and I've found that when these two emotions meet at a crossroads, water almost always comes to the surface. This got me wonderin'...

THE SETTING condensed is this: While eating at the Pharisee Simon's table, Jesus is tenderly cared for by a woman of dubious reputation. Knowing her background, Simon is amazed that Jesus has allowed this to continue, thinking to himself, "If this man were a real prophet, he would know who this woman is who touches him, and what sort of woman she is, a sinner."

Jesus answers his unspoken doubts with a parable of two men's debt to a moneylender. Both were unable to pay, but one's bill was ten times that of the other. Both are let off the hook. So, Jesus asks, which one should be more grateful?

The obvious answer offered by Simon is followed by a hands-on application of this lesson as demonstrated by the

hosting Pharisee and the present notorious woman. Her ser-
vice and sacrifice for Jesus far outshines Simon's, He sug-
gests, for with her many sins forgiven, a grateful heart is her
guide. Little forgiveness begets little love, Jesus concludes,
then sends her on her way forgiven and whole—a free
woman indeed!

As wonderful as this final lesson is, my first focus starts
earlier. It centers not so much on what the woman did as
where it was done. The text says she "learned that Jesus was
at table in the Pharisee's house." But surely this wasn't the
only place she could have run into him. Why did she pick a
place guaranteed to subject her to public ridicule? Couldn't
she have waited outside the door under the cover of darkness
(as Nicodemus did) to catch Him as He left? Why did she
choose a dining room full of condemnation for her confes-
sional box?

Let me suggest a possible answer with a memory picture
that came to me a few months back. Out of the blue one
morning, I remembered my father's vegetable garden.

When I was growing up, my father's garden was a yearly
testimony to his prolific green thumb. Carrots (my favorite
back then), beans, tomatoes, peas, beets, and squash popped
out of the ground by mid-August, putting the pictures on the
seed packets to shame.

Between the rabbits, woodchucks and a backyard full of
nearly naked neighborhood kids swimming in our pond,
there was never any shortage of workers for the harvest.
After a hard afternoon of swimming and horsing around,

those veggies just begged to be picked—so "bean breaks" were a frequent occurrence. Peas were popular too (though more work for less yield), but the real prize was the carrots.

Maybe that was because you had to work the hardest for them, and you never knew till you pulled them up what they were going to look like. Oh, you knew they'd be orange, but you couldn't tell from what was exposed—the greens and the very top of the carrot—what the rest looked like. What's more, there was some risk involved. A poorly prepared excavation could yield you a handful of carrot greens and a much harder extraction to follow.

The safest bet was to take your time and dig deep around the edge of the treasure so that you held onto more than stock when you gave a yank. The more root your hand held, the greater were your chances for getting a whole carrot. The question was never if you had the strength to pull it up, but whether you had enough purchase on the prize!

The same holds true for our Lord's Grace, doesn't it.

He can heal us to our very roots if we give Him enough of ourselves. The issue is never the strength in God's arm, but the grip we allow Him to get on our sin.

If we give it to Him, He will free us of the stock in our lives—while the roots of our travails persist. Our garden will look picked but will yield little in the fruit of a guilt-free life of joy. The more we honestly expose of our corrupted "carrot" to His merciful hand, the greater will be the harvest of His hope and healing at the very core of our lives.

Back to the woman in Luke and the question of why she chose to receive her absolution in front of her accusers.

Perhaps she knew the truth of a carrot's harvest. There could be no alibis in that room, no excuses. She could not hide who she had been and what she had done in any "stock" of pretense or situational ethics. She knew that they knew—and that very knowledge eliminated any hope of disguising her "root."

At that dinner party she was laid bare by the stares, whispers, and gasps. She was, as Simon quite correctly thought, "a sinner." She knew it only too well, and by her courageous presence there, she acknowledged it to the world.

As we all know, she was not the only sinner in the room; but very likely she was the only one the Lord's forgiveness could touch and heal at that time. She held nothing back, so Jesus was free to fully champion her life with His love. Gratitude flooded her heart and spilled onto His feet in tears. She had nothing to hide. She was released. And with her liberty came a love so large it anointed God.

That kind of freedom is appealing isn't it? But it's so costly! Must we publicly humiliate ourselves to gain the kind of all-encompassing pardon she received? Well, no, I don't believe public humiliation is the point. Honestly offering all our lies, deceptions, idols, compulsions, and games on the altar of God's merciful heart is. We must learn that nothing can be held back if we are to receive everything He wants to give us.

He will yank free our sin (and the oppressive hold it has on us) if we give Him enough of the "carrot" to get a good grip.

That exposure might very well cost us in pride and perceived esteem, but its price is cheap compared to the *priceless* freedom of the totally forgiven. Besides, as we all know, our coverups ain't cheap either! We've been paying their dues all our life and have precious little to show for it, except secrets, guilt, anger, and a low-level sense of dread and despair. Wasn't it T.S. Eliot who said, "Christianity is really very simple...Christ wants everything."

When I was a boy of ten, I stole a little green car from a bin at the local five-and-dime store. As foolish as that act was, to go from there to religion class was an even bigger blunder. (Or was it?) For there I heard in graphic detail by a substitute teacher, the horrors that awaited any and all offenders of God's most holy laws, the Ten Commandments. (I still think she spent an inordinate amount of time on THOU SHALT NOT STEAL!)

By the end of the class, I was in a panic, with that hot little car burning a hole in my guilty little pocket. I slunk home, avoiding all major highways for fear a tractor trailer would flatten me and send my black little soul down to Hades.

I stayed up in my room all weekend like some escaped convict in a deserted mountain cabin. I avoided all unnecessary contact with people, skipped meals, cried a lot, philosophized about the fickle nature of life and the irreversible consequences of the choices we make (I was a precocious child), and generally lived the miserable life of a man on the run. Finally by Sunday afternoon, my older brother had had enough of my whimpering, monosyllabic answers to his queries about what was wrong. He went to my parents.

"You've got to do something about the kid," he complained. "He's moping around the room, crying in his pillow and muttering something about, *They'll never take me alive!*"

Thankfully, my mother recognized repressed guilt when she saw it and came to the rescue. She then established what would become a family tradition. It was fundamentally a form of plea bargaining that was pulled out whenever the truth was too hard to admit. She called it "chat" and it went like this.

If you came to her and said "chat" and told her the truth, the-whole-truth-and-nothing-but-the-truth, of the awful thing you'd done, she would not get mad. She would forgive you and assure you that as soon as you asked God, He would do the same.

She didn't promise freedom from consequence—partly because that was not always hers to give and partly because she knew that the bitter taste of consequence can blessedly return at the gate of many a temptation. She did, however, promise (and deliver) plenty of hugs for your honesty—as well as the intoxicating pleasure of being known, "zits" and all, and still completely loved!

The only real rule to this wonderful bargain was complete and full exposure of your crime. No excuses or alibis, no circumstantial explanations to take the heat off of what you had done—just the ugly, bald truth of your sin. I think she knew that nothing less would ultimately alleviate the pain. And she was right.

Racked with grateful sobs, I pulled back my pillow to expose the horrid green four-wheeled source of my anguish. She knew almost without me having to explain what had transpired, and confiscated its diabolical little chassis before another teardrop hit the floor.

Sensing I'd suffered enough, she didn't make me bring it back (though I never saw it again either). Legalists may quibble at that decision, but I'm convinced it's not the point. Freedom—down to the shoes of my soul from the prison of my guilt, hidden lies and disguised disgraces—was. Thanks, Mom! And thank you Lord for Your message through her.

What was that message? Simply that Jesus is willing and most able to forgive anything we have done...no matter how big we think it is! We need only fully admit it and deeply regret it to allow Him access to our shame. And sometimes (perhaps even most times), He insures the completeness of our contrition by using another human being as an agent for His absolution.

The woman in Luke had Our Lord in person. For our time, we have His flesh and blood in the Body of Christ, His church, helping to affirm the truth of the last words in

Matthew's Gospel, *"And be assured I am with you always, to the end of time."*

Perhaps God is nudging you to unburden some secrets and shames that have dogged you like a curse your whole life. Jesus declared to the woman, *"Go in peace, your faith has saved you."* These are words He longs to say to you as well.

Is there some "car" under your pillow that keeps you from hearing these words in your own heart? Perhaps a confession to a loved one, spouse, or pastor is in order. Don't put it off. Tap the rich, limitless reservoir of grace God has availed to us by "coming clean" before the tender, merciful heart of Jesus. Then watch a lake of love spill out into your life as you bask in the sun of His forgiveness.

"I tell you her great love proves that her many sins have been forgiven."

The Lies of the Eyes

"I'm dying," he said to the chaplain intern,
then a cough came so deep the hall nurse returned.
"Lean over here boy, hurry for God's sake,
I've got too little time and a confession to make."
He kicked the girl out and raised up his bed,
then stared at the ceiling till he seemed almost dead.
And as his strength disappeared and his eyes slowly sank,
rivers of tears ran over the bank.

"When I was a boy on my way home from school,
I'd stop by a brook where the rocks made a pool.
I'd kneel at its edge like some foreign guest
and drink from a cup of fingers and flesh.
Then one afternoon by an old exposed root,
a magazine lay like a forbidden fruit.
All of my Eden-youth died in a stare.
All of my fleeing truth started there.

Never had I seen persons undress
then mingle in pleasure and purposelessness.
Never were faces so free from their shame,
flaunting and fearless impervious to pain.
Women so naked I blushed while alone,
though enjoying a renegade warmth in my bones.
I was abased and abandoned to a new appetite
that powerfully masqueraded as light.
That's where the secrets all seemed to begin
from family to lovers and all other friends.
A spy so disguised in a cold carnal war,
for years I would hide what I said I abhorred.
Under cover by day with a wife and a child,
a job and a home and a suburban smile,
I'd cruise the nights lined in "adult" arcades,
Dr. Jekyll and Hyde in a private parade.

When a lie is a life two choices remain,
to die with your strife or renounce it by name.
But like any old habit it was hard to let go
so the death that I chose was deceptively slow.
Family and friends were all part of its toll,
as slowly the decency drained from my soul.
Further and harder and colder I'd go,
till I was all by myself with the video.

Injecting disease that I kept out of sight,
sticking it into my heart like a knife.

So what you see here is the corpse of a man,
dead by indulgence at his very own hand.

The lies of the eyes are a shadow of shame
That eats your insides like a worm in the brain.
A legion of lust that haunts in the heart
And tells you you must while it tears you apart.
Though it's too late for me, you must realize
The death I can see in the lies of the eyes."

Then he looked at the cleric so hard and so long
Embarrassed, the young man broke into a song...
"Amazing Grace how sweet the sound"...
Somewhere near the end the man's head
slumped down.

Mercy, God's Wild Card

REMEMBER "WILD CARDS" in your rainy-summertime-afternoon-with-nothing-much-to-do days? At first, just the "Jokers" were wild, but as the rain continued and boredom got the upper hand, you expanded the magic to deuces and one-eyed Jacks.

The premise was simple. A wild card could be anything you wanted it to be, needed it to be, at the present moment. It broke open any game, and ravaged its rules. Just as you were about to be counted out, a wild card could reverse the verdict. The purists, of course, called it cheating (particularly if it thwarted their victory) but all appreciated its illogical leverage in a jam.

So it is with mercy. It makes no sense—and often seems to invalidate the existing laws. (Remember the woman caught in adultery? "In the Law Moses has laid down that such women are to be stoned. What do you say about it?") Yet it is a wild card played from the very heart of God. Again and again Jesus pulled it out in matters of heart over head, love over law. Again and again in words and actions the Son of God and Man proclaimed the irrational truth of His

Father's heart as spoken through the prophets, "I require mercy, not sacrifice."

A kind of guarded skepticism has often surrounded my thoughts concerning this most reckless of God's attributes. It sure is nice of Him, all right, to keep on loving and forgiving long after a guilty party deserves such treatment. It is most gracious of God to be the voice crying in our wilderness *"give 'em another chance,"* when the worldly jury comes back with death in their eyes. But is it wise? Could liberal dispensing of mercy breed the kind of sinner who would chronically abuse the favor? Would too much of this good thing create the sort of person who could use the mercy of God eventually as a built-in absolution for everything? One should certainly be loving, but after a while couldn't that quality degenerate to dangerous irresponsibility as well? I mean, where do you draw the line? Where does the consequence for our actions come into it?

Though I am sure these warnings have often come true, it is fascinating (to say nothing of ironic) that Jesus' actions here on earth many times answered such cautions with a bold, emphatic, "I'm gonna be merciful anyway."

What I have often overlooked in my judgmental zeal is that true mercy has little or nothing to do with the consequence of actions. Thank God! Except for our refusal to accept and receive His mercy (He won't violate my will's free choice to reject His love), God has an unending, unlimited, unconditional supply of compassion and forgiveness for all our rebellious, sinful actions.

What! Sin without consequence! No, no, not at all. There is, of course, always a consequence to every violation of God's law and will. Sometimes it is painfully obvious. Often, however, we are unaware of it in any measurable way. But whether I feel it or not has nothing to do with Our Lord's dispensation of mercy. For mercy has much more to do with His unchangeable opinion of me than with my ability to perceive, receive or deceive the consequence of sin.

I've noticed that when I view with suspicion the liberal use of mercy on a flagrant transgressor, I'm often more concerned with the injustice of his eluding retribution ("He shouldn't get away with that!") than with the misuse or abuse of Divine kindliness. It's the why-do-evil-men-prosper kind of stuff.

What I have only recently come to see is that mercy is ultimately not a tool of judgment, to be dispensed or withheld in response to our behavior, but a free choice of a loving God originating from His tender heart.

The concern that a theology with mercy at its center might be too lenient to the incessant sinner misses the whole heart of the subject, which is simply this: The wild card of mercy is a characteristic of God—not just one of the many ministry arrows in His quiver. It is who He is, not just simply a description of what He so frequently does. In other words, it's part of His definition, not a partial explanation of His occupation.

This is an immensely important differentiation for the frequently fallen saint, as it puts to death, once and for all, the mistaken idea that mercy's flow is somehow controlled by our actions (as if we could at some point push God over the brink by our behavior). If mercy were anything less than a primal character trait of our Lord, this might be so. But again, it is more His nature than His theology, more like the leopard's spots than the leopard's disposition. Hard as it may be to believe, God will be merciful to you whether you are Mother Teresa or Adolf Hitler. There is nothing we can do to change His nature, which is to love us unconditionally.

Understanding this is helpful in the believer's lifelong task of loving sinners not their sin—particularly when dealing with the sinner in oneself. I believe Peter never knew himself nor the true depth of Jesus' love until he looked into His face with that third curse barely free of his lips. No defenses, no alibis, no excuses—just the bald, bare shell of a frightened little man after all the boasting had died down. We need to stand in Peter's shoes. To learn what Peter learned that night. To understand that mercy is a road into the heart of God that is only walked by sinners.

It is not the healthy that need a doctor, but the sick;
I did not come to invite virtuous people, but sinners.

Mercy as God's wild card certainly tells us much about who He is. It is also, moreover, a major clue about how we're to be. For it is a flower that only blossoms in the soil of our acknowledged sin. We will not see its beauty nor smell its forgiving fragrance until we honestly look at ourselves. We—pauper-poor with no attributes but our annoying tendency to promise what we can't deliver—must truthfully stare into the face of Jesus. Only then will we begin to understand the marvelous message in His mercy, which was, is and always will be "I love you . . . regardless."

There is an ancient prayer that has kept the body and soul of sainted sinners together since the beginning of the church. Everything previously said here could easily be forgotten if these few words might linger in your heart.

LORD JESUS CHRIST, SON OF THE LIVING GOD, HAVE MERCY ON ME, A SINNER.

VII

Time Wonders / Now Knowings

*The only way you'll be refused
is if you say "No"
to "Yes."*

When the Sun Comes Out

Day to day the overcasting gray of damaged dreams
Hangs above our fragile broken love or so it seems.
Just beneath the smiles, a lonely grief clings shadow close.
Just behind the brag a malaised mind haunts you like a ghost.
And you cry out, and try out yet a new despair.
But it's lonesome and peace won't come.
And sadness sinks to fear.

Through the door of mercy's metaphor an image fills the fray.
Old as light following the night, new as everlasting day.
Love has hung, like an ever-faithful sun
in the higher heaven's blue.
Though it hides behind shame-filled cloudy skies
the light is waiting there for you.
So you break down, and take down the idols of your ache.
As you fall back, you call back the hope that always waits.

*WHEN THE SUN COMES OUT AND SPILLS ITS YELLOW YES
ON THE JEWELRY OF THE LAWN
THERE'S A HOPE THAT SHOUTS DEEP WITHIN THE BREAST
LIKE A NIGHT THAT'S COMING INTO DAWN.*

Could it be this simple mystery of hide and seek
Holds a clue deep in the heart of WHO
that makes the truth complete?
For once there hung an ever-faithful Son
from the gallows of our grief.
Yet still today His goodness gobbles gray and buoys up belief.
So come on, come on, hold on to the wounded hand of grace.
Though in dark's doubt, lay your heart out.
Feel your chill this love replace.

A Problem Parable

Most of Jesus' parables appeal to me. Quite predictably, I assume I'm the "good guy" in them (or at least it is my desire to be). I like to think of myself as more Samaritan- than Levi-like on the whole. So, for instance, when reading the parable of The Good Samaritan, it's not personally confusing as to whom I should emulate. Of course, whether I actually behave like that merciful traveler all the time is another matter.

There are, however, a few teaching stories of Jesus that do not lend themselves to such an easy affiliation with right and renunciation of wrong. In these brief allegories, the ethical and theological landscape usually is not a gray area for Jesus. He is His usual adamant self, etching out the parameters of a divine truth with the notorious authority and lucidity of the only Son of God.

I, on the other hand, am often squirming and internally troubled by them. The reason is probably obvious. Without any effort at all, I find myself cheering for the bad guy, the very one our Savior is probably admonishing. Whoops!

A good case in point can be found in the Gospel of Matthew, the first sixteen verses. In brief summation, a vineyard owner starts hiring laborers at the crack of dawn for a long day's work. The first workers agree on a fair wage and begin their toil. Throughout the day the landowner employs others for what one assumes are similar tasks. He promises to remunerate each new group fairly for their efforts. At day's end he pays all the same amount he agreed to give the first hired. This decision, as one might imagine, is received with mixed reviews.

Not wishing to take anything out of anyone's pocket, a representative for the first hired does not ask for the later hired to receive less, but that the early shift, having put in a much fuller day, might receive more than what the original contract stipulated.

The "boss man" disagrees with this logic for two basic reasons. First, he has not broken his part of the bargain with anyone and therefore is not obliged to pay more; and second, the money is his to do with as he chooses. He then concludes the discussion by advising the indignant worker to keep his "green" in check. "Why be jealous because I am kind?"

Jesus than wraps up the whole affair in those familiar words, "Thus will the last be first and the first last."

Today such a case would be a "juicy steak" for most union or affirmative action lawyers. A clear situation of preferential treatment and economic discrimination in the workplace. The ethnic background, gender and sexual preference of the slighted workers might even be scrutinized to see if a civil rights violation or two were hiding someplace. Before it was over, the landowner would likely have to sell his place to pay for the emotional damages incurred by the plaintiff (to say nothing of the cost of his own legal fees).

Yep, our skin's a lot thinner these days in such matters; (and perhaps you share, to greater or lesser degree, my sense of overkill with it all). We are "put out" mighty easily of late. What did *Time* magazine recently call us, "a nation of crybabies." And yet,something *is* quite understandable about that vineyard worker's complaint.

Yeah, yeah the landowner is legally within his rights, but ethically he sure seems kind of cold. I mean, according to the tale, he pays all the late arrivals first in front of the early birds. Tact is clearly not one of his strong suits. And there isn't even any indication of some verbal appreciation directed toward the first workers.

All this may not be required behavior in the workplace, but it sure is preferred—and it would seem appropriate. So call it a feeling. It just feels like the employer could have acted more humanely... been a tad more sensitive... shown a little more fairness in his dealings.

It's also easy to have a greater sympathy for the other son's complaint in the prodigal's parable. Doesn't it seem in either story that the hard-working, faithful and loyal person in the situation is almost overlooked and his rebellious or late-arrived counterpart is rewarded for his vice or deficiency? *Hmmm.* Bothersome and curious. Not an easy lesson at all. A real problem parable!

Still, Jesus clearly sides with the owner in this story. And, because I've learned to trust His actions and opinions over my feelings (well, most of the time!), I decided, upon rereading this passage recently, to linger awhile. Two previously unrealized thoughts came to the surface.

The first was alarmingly personal—and yet, because I saw it in the context of my life, I understood its truth quickly and deeply. Simply put, I noticed that the first worker's disenchantment was directly linked to his distracting fascination with and inordinate interest in the other workers' relationships to the boss. This came into unsettling clarity as I pondered a similar circumstance in my own life. Let me explain.

For many years, dear and well meaning friends and faithful listeners of my music have voiced a repeated complaint to me in touchingly urgent sincerity:

"Why don't more people know about your music?"

"How come you don't get better airplay?"

"I think your stuff is a hundred times better than some of the junk that's out there. Why do the radio people play that schlock and not yours?"

As flattering as these questions have been to my ego, I (not wishing to tarnish my well-polished "just a servant" persona) have, in pseudo-humility, usually responded with something like, "Well...in God's time" or "If He wills it so."

I've even aligned my creative output with the ignominy and stigma of the Cross as an explanation for exclusion from mass popularity. (No problem of withering ego here!) The uncomfortable truth is that I didn't need anybody to form such questions in my mind. I've been internally asking them for twenty years!

"Hey, God! I've been out in these here musical 'fields' since before daybreak. I've been, to quote the man in the parable, sweating 'the whole day long in the blazing sun!' I've been working hard at this thing, with not many grumbles (at least in public) all the days of my adult life, and who do you 'bless' with high visibility and runaway prosperity but some young punk who can barely find his way out of the key of C."

Well, it didn't take very long, when viewed from the inside out, for me to see the flaw in the "faithful" worker's argument. Put in my own personal context, those words hung in my mouth like bad breath. How ugly and unseemly, how boastful and arrogant. How full of "me" and absent of gratitude. How self-absorbed and self-directed.

But more importantly, the personal context helped me see how profoundly untrue they were as well. It became only too clear that God never promised any of the things I whined about being denied. We made a deal years ago in the spring of our love about the things I could and couldn't do, should and shouldn't do, and I was honored He picked me for a small portion of a marvelous task He had planned.

From the very start, I felt His pleasure in my creative efforts and meanderings, but never more acutely than in the real blood, sweat, and tears of the "doing it"—the work itself. The partnership of the project was my true lasting joy and ecstasy. Yet early out, I began to gripe and worry about who else was working the street and where I was in comparison to them. I began to take my eyes off my First Love and put them on a false love.

God was and is forgiving of me in this. He has not, however, backed off from his original arrangement. How many times have I sensed Him saying while I paced the floor waiting for the world to recognize the gift, *Get back to work! Leave the phone alone! I'll make it ring if and when I want to...I gave you the gift, now stick to the deal...Come on, let's you and I get back to work.*

It was drifting from the original agreement that bred the infection of discontent in the first worker. And that disease was contracted the moment he took his eyes off his own intimate contract (relationship) with his master.

Point One is summed up for me in the chorus of one of my most favorite hymns.

TURN YOUR EYES UPON JESUS
LOOK FULL IN HIS WONDERFUL FACE
AND THE THINGS OF EARTH WILL GROW STRANGELY DIM
IN THE LIGHT OF HIS GLORY AND GRACE.

Point Two came to me later and is perhaps more theoretical in its scope than humanly practical in its application; but I think it bears mentioning.

This parable was an analogy for the kingdom of heaven. It describes the kind of clean air God would have us breathe, in contrast to the polluted sludge we're often spiritually gulping. What became very clear to me is that in God's country, the concepts we hold so dear—first and last, fastest and slowest, smartest and dumbest, richest and poorest—are, quite frankly, irrelevant. They simply don't make God's list of what's important.

Applying this parable in modern terms: seniority is not in God's vocabulary. The issue with God is never how much time we've put in, compared to someone else—lest we think we can **earn** His approval and affection and view ourselves in some elevated standing with Him—but rather, *what is the present health of our focus on and relationship with Him?*

Are we evaluating our lot by the blessings we perceive others are receiving from God...entrusting our peace to the fickle and jealous god of comparison? Isn't that truly none of our business? Not only will that breed the frustrations of the first hired worker, it's not the central point God wishes to make.

When He says the first shall be last and the last first, I doubt He's sending out a call for all front-runners to drop back (as if by becoming last you'll really be first in His book). That would merely usher in a new age of programmed paint-by-numbers humility.

Isn't He perhaps suggesting that "last" and "first" are "un-terms" with Him? Meaningless to the real concern He has for our everlasting partnership.

Yes, by all means, practice humility and a servant-like attitude in all you do, but not because it will garner you any backward status points in God's peculiar system of merit which has the losers somehow winners. Do it because it will clarify your vision of Jesus and how loved you are by Him. With Him in view and a "beyond knowing" knowledge of His affection for us in our hearts, little else matters. What more could we possibly long for at the end of our days than to hear, *"Well done, my good and faithful servant"* whispered in the secret work chamber of our heart after a lifetime of quiet, side-by-side labor and love.

My ways are not your ways, My thoughts are not your thoughts, God says through His prophet Isaiah. So since we can't possibly understand Him—and how and why He does the things He does—perhaps we'd do well spending less time figuring out the "unfigurable" and more time back in the shop with the Boss getting our little part of His Kingdom built.

The View Out the Window

$\mathcal{A}$ FEW YEARS AGO, while on the road in the Midwest, I was awakened from an afternoon snooze by the sound of geese flying low and honking loud very close to my motel window.

Pressing my face to every corner of the glass, I discovered to my great disappointment and minor frustration that whatever part of the sky they were inhabiting, it wasn't visible from my room. In short, on that day I had to be content to hear the song of their travels without viewing their evocative "chevron flight." Nothing new to that, of course.

It used to happen to me off and on as a boy growing up in the 50's. Back then, however, it was with helicopters, not wild geese. I remember one long spring I was pretty much bedridden with anemia. I'd hear the chopper coming off in the distance. (That "a-wucka-pucka-wucka-pucka" sound was so distinctive.)

Up against the window I'd squeeze my face hoping to get a glimpse of what was back then a rare occurrence. The sound got louder, my eyes got bigger, the searching harder, but often I couldn't find it in the sky—though from the sheer racket I was almost sure it was landing on the roof.

Soon the propeller sound would start to fade and I knew that, at least today, it wasn't gonna happen. As with the geese, I had to accept the fact that though there was plenty of sky out the window, it wasn't the whole sky. In truth, it probably wasn't even half of it.

Though my ears told me I should be able to read the numbers on the belly of the whirlybird or touch the wings of those high honkers, I saw nothing. For you see, the view out the window is just a piece of the sky.

The longer I live, the more useful and comforting a simple metaphor like this is to me. For more and more these days, I'm convinced of the profound limitations in my perceptions, particularly with things spiritual.

When I look out my faith's window, though I might daily try to wash and clean its glass, increasingly there is much that is outside the vision of my belief's understanding... much for which my theology has no neat, clean answer. That, by the way, is not always so much the fault of the window as a characteristic of the sky.

Children know this difficulty in their perceptions so very well. There is a request that makes perfect sense to a child. From the kid's-eye-view it could be easily granted by either Mom or Dad. In fact, the only reason it wouldn't be allowed is out-and-out meanness, or so their view seems to logically conclude. Yet for reasons larger than their immediate perceptions and greater than the predictable pain of their disappointment, the request is denied. The only close-to-accurate explanation coming from on high is a somewhat hollow sounding, "Someday you'll understand!"

The spurned child neither understands nor wants to wait for "someday." Their "window" cannot presently expand to see the larger picture. That's just the way it is. The child must trust that the parent's unpopular decision is driven by love, no matter how hard it is to understand. Ultimately, children are healthier knowing they were deprived of some desired thing because of love than feeling they were granted it out of apathy or neglect.

So it is too for all our grown-up questions, misunderstandings, hurts and heartaches—whose answers, or at least explanations, seem to be just beyond the rim of understanding.

We could conclude like hurt and disappointed children that such out-of-our-reach knowledge is the product of a capricious, mean-spirited Maker who could have prevented our misery but didn't. Or maybe that our misfortunes and heartaches are just the result of a series of hapless, unconnected, miserable moments.

How much richer we are, though, and freer from bitterness when we entrust our unknowns to a larger Love rather than a darker indifference or cosmic luck-of-the-draw. Ironic, isn't it, that at precisely the point we might be tempted to throw in the towel where the larger, harder-to-understand love of God is concerned, we are ever more in need of trusting Him. A child needs a hand to hold all the more when walking in the dark.

This is why throughout the Bible when hard "why" or "how-come" or "when-will-ya" or "where-will-ya" questions are asked of God, He invariably responds to them with Himself. For He knows that though we crave answers, we fundamentally need Him. Not as the "Answer Man" or "Mr. Fixit," but as the Lover of our soul, the One whose love we can count on, trust in, through and beyond our misunderstandings, confusions or unanswered questions.

Throughout our journey it behooves us more and more, therefore, to know God as a child knows his parent, with intuitive trust and reckless abandon.‡ For be assured, there is much in this life we won't understand. Not now... not later... maybe not ever.

The little we know of heaven from Scripture has never portrayed it as a celestial encyclopedia for life's toughest questions. No, all we can be assured of is that the One who loves us will be there. I've got a hunch that when the time comes, that'll be enough.

---

‡*I know how destructive this picture can be to a child who was abused. If that, dear reader, is your story, substitute for "parent" the one or two people in your life whose love has earned your trust.*

Have You Practiced "Yes" Today?

"There is a photograph of you..." starts a song about my wife I wrote several years ago. I had asked her what she wanted for her approaching birthday and Greta sheepishly replied, "Well, a song would be nice."

I felt a certain pang of guilt with this request for no such tuneful testimony of my affection had been forthcoming since we dated well over a decade earlier. It is, I regret, not uncommon for me to frequently overlook this major cornerstone of my emotional stability.

I started the song immediately. Soon after beginning it, a favorite photograph of Greta came to mind. It had been taken the first year of our marriage—a time when she was working as an elementary school teacher, helping to put me through school. (I'm a chronic late bloomer.)

The picture caught her one morning on the porch steps outside our apartment with books in hand heading off to her class. Somehow that impromptu portrait captured the hope, energy and commitment I've come to know in the woman.

To anyone else, it was probably just a picture of a pretty young girl with an armful of books. But to me, it was so much more. I wrote the song in a couple of hours. It was an easy task with such a fertile visual base.

Interestingly enough, as I was mulling over the thoughts for this article while jogging the other day (not a pretty sight by the way... how come everyone else looks so together and unruffled and, well, sweatless when they run?) another picture of Greta came to mind. And once again, from its image, mountains of applicable material popped into my head.

She was probably three years old when it was taken, playing outside her parents' home in Detroit. As the shutter snapped, she gave one of her still famous smiles. It was simply bursting with what might be described as the affirmation of being—or put more succinctly, *YES! YES! And again I say YES! YES to life. YES to my shoes. YES to the grass. YES to my tricycle. YES to this day, this hour, this minute, this very second... YES! YES! YES!*

We're built for "YES," aren't we? Oh sure, we do "NO" pretty well, but we have to learn it, practice it. "YES" comes naturally. It's our first choice, our primary inclination if nothing else gets in the way to convince us otherwise.

Watch some kids playing unthreatened and unintimidated, free to follow each possibility their imaginations present to them. Why, they're almost the very incarnation of the word. And that I believe is as it should be.

It is the most basic character trait of our Author coming from out of our nature—as well as, I believe, a primal question waiting for an answer. Not only "YES!" but "YES?" From early on we ask it to our parents, our playmates, our teachers . . . why, even the postman for goodness' sake!

"Isn't life great? Yes? Isn't it fun? Yes? Don't ya want to play with me? Huh, don't ya? Can you come over and play with me now . . . can ya?"

And yet for many, probably most, that instinctive "YES" is gradually converted to "NO." No greater case can be made for the influence of "the Fall" on humans than the slow, methodical transformation of a life from its early, innate optimism to its later grimly pragmatic, worldly-wise, pessimism.

Again and again our innocent "YES?" questions have been answered with a cautious, careful, well-constructed and thought-out, very adult, "Not now," or "Don't be silly," or "Can't you see I'm busy," or "You'll understand when you're older."

Loosely translated, all those answers sift down to a resounding "NO." It doesn't happen overnight and it doesn't happen in a vacuum—but it does happen.

Once again, some photographs I recently came across helped to bring this into focus for me. They were several old photos of the same person. All were dated and showed in snapshots her life from a child through middle age.

Seen through these small installments of captured moments, a dramatic change in her overall countenance was quite apparent. It probably was nowhere near as obvious to those who knew her day-to-day, but as mini-signposts to a lifetime, the transformation was most unsettling. If verbally articulated, each photo in succession might have read something like this.

1902, Yes! 1909, Yes... I think so. 1912, Yes... I hope so. 1916, Uh huh... I guess so. 1920, Oh, I don't know... maybe.

1925, I don't know. 1929, I kind of doubt it. 1934, What do you want?! 1937, I don't know... No! Now stop bothering me!

1939, No!

In varying degrees I imagine we all can relate to this slow slide to "No." We might avoid its truth and deny its reality, but we cannot escape the toll it takes on our spirit, or scars it leaves on our heart, or hope it robs from our eyes. It is a sad, bad joke if life is left here... simply to "slip slide away" as Paul Simon has said.

But then, of course for many, the cavalry arrives (or is it Calvary?)... always, it would seem, just in the nick of time. His name is Jesus. In a marvelous, quite impossible to describe way, His great "YES" answers our feeble little one, denouncing and renouncing all the "No's" that have polluted our days.

It's called conversion, rebirth, renewal and many other things. It is our heart's first cry, finally being answered in Person by its very Author. It is a wonder beyond words... the very reason we were created.

Rebirth is an apt description of it, for our hearts are once again as full of "YES" as when we were children. But unlike before, we learn "YES's" other name: FAITH . . . the marvelous and mysterious connecting of God's "YES" with ours.

And once the merger of these affirmations takes place in our innermost chamber, it forms a bond that nothing, at any time, in any place, can ever break up. If you don't believe me, read Romans chapter 8, verses 37 to 39. Verbal super glue!

It is a surprise to no one that this wonderful melding of hopes, this communion of "YES's" eventually takes some organized form or structure. Let's call it the religion of "YES." As such, this is neither good nor bad. It's just a fact.

But, of course, the religion of anything is not the thing itself—just as being a baseball fan is not the same thing as playing baseball. It's fine to be in the stands cheering, but it's no substitute for being *in the game.* Religion is the structure that develops around "YES" (i.e. FAITH), and, as such, if it helps to continually reacquaint us with the Source, the Author, it can be quite useful.

Often, however, we find it's easier to participate and practice the religion of something like "YES" rather than perpetually confront its Author and mingle our "YES" with His. The reason is obvious. It's safer, less taxing, and plays into our tenacious tendency to hide from the truth and run with rebellion. We frequently buy off our behavior with a rationale sounding something like this:

Hey, how far off could I be if I stick to the rules of the religion. I mean, they're based on that original "YES" I heard, right?

The flaw in this sort of logic shows up in the snapshot of the first "YES," that initial affirming exuberance. You see, the kid calling that "YES" and hearing it answered, never grows up. Call it the Peter Pan factor of faith, if you will. When will you ever become an adult of God? (Oh what an awful thought!) You will always be a child of God—and that child will always need to hear from the SOURCE, not just the religion built up around Him.

But it is right at this point where the next slow, subtle, slip-sliding away to "No" can take root. It's kind of like a spiritual heart disease that slowly, over time, debilitates. I call it the **Slow Stroke of Despair (SSOD)**, and it can, if un-detected, squeeze the "YES" right out of a believer's life.

It's usually nothing obvious at first—for we still talk a good "YES," sing a good "YES," even, in some cases, preach a good "YES." But we slowly forget how to be "YES"...how to abide in "YES" like the little girl in the photo, or the new convert.

"YES" is intellectualized or theologicalized (how's that for a new word?!). But it's not actualized. "YES" is something that, if not actualized, will change—gradually, perhaps, but it will happen.

Like the snapshots of that person's life on any given day, you won't see a difference, but over time, it'll be there. Just talking about "YES" won't stave off this deterioration (though you're likely to believe it does). Eventually, with this **SSOD**, our child-heart "YES" muscles atrophy till they seem useless and silly—almost an embarrassment or insult to our more realistic and pragmatic intellect. The classic symptom is the mind accusing the heart of childishness and then taking over the very control and use of "YES."

Most of the central characters created by novelist Graham Greene are afflicted with this disease—so much so that one suspects they are all in some way autobiographical etchings of a heart that has fallen out of favor with a head. It is the childish (or is it child-like?) "YES" of faith meeting (and usually being overrun by) the grown-up "No" of logic and the grit of the way-things-really-are.

The worst part about this stroke is that we don't really know it's happening most of the time. Its paralysis takes place in the part of us which society and, yes, even the church sometimes condemns as juvenile and beneath our intellectual potential.

We are led to believe and, eventually convinced, that this affliction is natural, necessary, inevitable—even part of the maturing process as responsible adults.

That's a lie! That something happens frequently and to many does not make it correct; it only makes it common. But remember, a common disease is no less a disease just because it's common.

The tragedy here is that it is a curable disease—curable through constant rehabilitation, that is. Just as with a physical stroke, the victims of the **Slow Stroke of Despair** need a regimen of steady, daily therapy to regain the use of their traumatized natural and divine "YES" muscles. It takes practice, practice and more practice. We must practice being and living and abiding in "YES".

But how? Let me close with two brief suggestions.

First: activate the Peter Pan principle of faith in your devotional life. What devotional life? Okay, okay so maybe it's been awhile. That's probably another symptom of the **SSOD**.

Throughout the life of a believer, it is periodically imperative to reconnect our primal child-like "YES" to Jesus—not just as an exercise in getting back to basics, but as a life-giving reaffirmation of our primary status as a much loved child of God.

It's an issue, really, of trust. A child does not trust with his intellect but with his heart. He does not trust a concept or an organization but a Person. He needs more than documents (however inspired) to assure him of that Person's love. He needs hugs! That's what a devotional life brings to the believer. The daily opportunity to be hugged by Jesus. Take time to thank and adore, sit with and abide in, read about and meditate on, talk and listen to, and, yes, fall into the unconditional "YES" of Jesus Christ.

"With Him it was, and is, Yes. He is the Yes pronounced upon God's promises, everyone of them." (2 Corinthians 1:20).

Second: give feet to the communion of "YES" that resides in your heart. Apply your heart's "YES" in action, submitting it to the mandates and unctions of love. Remember, the re-learning and re-training of our "YES" muscles is brought about by practicing "YES" in a host of human ways, seeing the moments of your day as "YES" or "No" possibilities.

Often we relegate faith decisions only to those "spiritual" or "religious" times in our life, improperly segregating a great deal of our existence into sacred and secular categories. But when faith is synonymous with "YES," it enters all walks, stages, and circumstances of our journey, and grows the flowers of God in previously untilled fields.

Maybe someone at work needs a "YES" in the form of your listening ear, or your child does in the form of a good-night gab or unexpected side trip for an ice cream cone, or your spouse does with an unsolicited tender word or hug, or perhaps a difficult relationship needs it with your understanding and compassion. Wherever, it won't take long before you're seeing place after place that your gentle "YES" can replace the common and expected "No."

St. Paul wrote in his letter to the Galatians that "the only thing that counts is faith expressing itself through love" (5:6, NIV). Perhaps our walk is simpler than we think. Maybe it's just exchanging the word "faith" with "YES" in our day-to-day lives, practicing "YES" moment-by-moment.

In his marvelous little book, *The Great Divorce,* C. S. Lewis suggests that when a busload of hell-bound souls get one last chance to go to heaven, they all but one refuse the offer after a brief visit to the celestial city. Why? Because it only offered them "YES" and all their lives they'd practiced "No." It simply was not that appealing to them. Old habits die hard and, if we're not careful, sometimes they don't die at all.

Ironically, it was not a carriage full of hedonistic pagans on the bus. In fact, a good many of the souls were quite religious. None of them were kicked out of heaven. They walked out under their own steam . . . not God's choice but theirs.

Lewis later wrote that ultimately we say to God, "Thy will be done," or He reluctantly has to say to us "thy will be done." *HAVE YOU PRACTICED "YES" TODAY?*

Have You Practiced "Yes" Today?

Have you practiced "Yes" today
Peeked some blue sky through the gray
Stuck a smile to what you say to face a frown of fear?
Or nervous have you practiced "No"
Shut a door, closed down a show
Told an aching heart to go find another ear?

Have you practiced "Yes" today
Looked for goodness on the way
Interwove your work with play to keep the child alive?
Or darkened have you practiced "No"
Let the seeds of sadness sow
Helped the hopeless habits grow, dynasties inside?

FOR IN THE FINAL FRAME OF THINGS.
WHEN STANDING AT THE DOOR,
THE ONLY KEYS UPON OUR RING
WILL BE THE ONES WE'VE USED BEFORE.

Have you practiced "Yes" tonight
In the darkness laughed its light
Taken time to make things right, before you turn the page?
Or angry have you practiced "No"
Let icy winds of bitter blow
Hid your heart deep in the snow of unforgiven rage?

Have you practiced "Yes" tonight
Spoke it with a hug so tight
Wrapped it in a kiss good night, then washed it down
with prayer?
Or busy have you practiced "No"
Forgot that love is tell and show
Overlooked how fast they grow and that soon they
won't be there?

Let the children come to me,
The Son of God said once so tenderly.
For in these little ones I see my Father's loving will.
Yes, in our country all you need
Is simply the will to believe
That "Yes" is why you were conceived and, yes,
I love you still.

FOR IN THE FINAL WIN OR LOSE,
THE TRUTH NO MORE, NO LESS,
THE ONLY WAY YOU'LL BE REFUSED
IS IF YOU SAY "NO" TO "YES."

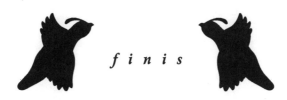

finis

Notes

Wildflower *Front cover photo*	One of the humblest flower flags gracing the New England summer roadside, Blue Chicory has always been a personal favorite. (I even wrote a song with that name for a long ago forgotten album.) Such simple beauty shining out from its weed status qualifies it perfectly for a visual complement to the title.
Magi *Page 22*	T.S. Eliot also tilled this field. When the waves of wealth came back over this altered little shore would the Jewel washed up on it still remain?
Jesus, Rightful Heir... *Page 26ff*	*Your father Abraham...was glad.* John 8:56 *In very truth...I am.* John 8:58
Bridget *Page 44*	Bridget was my father's mother. I know her only through my father's loving memory, as she died the year before he married. She was a world class mimic, says he, able to figure out any accent or dialect in an instant. In that way, though she has long since gone to her reward, I see her daily in my two children, Esther and Reuben, who share the same astounding gift.
Benimire's Stream *Page 44*	A favorite old song of the Blanchard family.

Love Has Faces
Page 111

Two stories that intertwine at the crossroads of compassion. Musically, the two choruses were designed to be sung together in duet fashion.

The Last Days
of a Daffodil
Page 115

A true testimony to the fact that AIDS is an equal opportunity heartbreaker, and that the Mercy and Grace of God are alive and well in the midst of this plague.

There Is a Wounding
Page 117

Scriptural text: Luke 7:36-50

Change of the Guard
Page 119

What God has joined together over fifty years ago let no man or disease tear apart.

Loneliness, Part 1
Page 135

"Jesus, my crucified Captain" from the song, *Lord of the Living,* on my album, BE YE GLAD, Diadem Music, 1989.

Loneliness, Part 2
Page 141

My thoughts...your ways. Isaiah 55:8

If Lydia Were Here
Page 148

One of the greatest proofs of the soul's existence is our imagination's ability to picture "her" years from now.

Mercy,
God's Wild Card
Page 168ff

In the law...about it? John 8:5
It is not...sick. Matthew 9:12
I did not...sinners. Matthew 9:13

Problem Parable
Page 177

Turn Your Eyes Upon Jesus
by Helen Howarth Lemmel
Copyright © 1922, Renewed 1950
Singspiration, Inc. All rights reserved.

Discography

Albums of
Michael Kelly Blanchard

QUAIL, *Gotz Records, 1977*

LOVE LIVES ON, *Gotz Records, 1980*

A COMMON THREAD, *Gotz Records, 1983*

MICHAEL KELLY BLANCHARD IN CONCERT,
Gotz Records, 1985

THE ATTIC TAPES, *Gotz Records, 1986*

HEART GUARD (Original Soundtrack), *Gotz Records, 1987*

THE HOLY LAND OF THE BROKEN HEART,
Gotz Records, 1988

BE YE GLAD, SONGS OF MICHAEL KELLY BLANCHARD,
Diadem Music, 1989

MERCY IN THE MAZE, *Diadem Music, 1991*

A VIEW OUT THE WINDOW, *Diadem Music, 1994*

Other Artists Covering MKB Songs

Be Ye Glad	Acappella, Debbie Boone, GLAD, Phil Driscoll, Noel Paul Stookey
Celebrate (Good News)	GLAD
Coast to Coast	Noel Paul Stookey
Danny's Downs	George King, Peter, Paul and Mary, Noel Paul Stookey
Great is the Lord God	Steve Green
The Love of the Father	GLAD, George King
Then the Quail Came	Peter Campbell (Australia), Noel Paul Stookey, Manfred Ziebald (Germany)

About Quail Ministries

FOUNDED IN 1985, Quail Ministries, Inc. is a non-profit ministry which seeks to be a tool in the belt of the divine carpenter, Jesus Christ. Its goal is to help replace our pain and loneliness with the heart-healing love of God through song, storytelling, drama, teaching, and writing.

A Common Thread

A free, biannual newsletter, A COMMON THREAD includes articles, lyrics, concert and retreat news, and updates on Quail Ministries. Most of the articles and some of the lyrics appearing in UNSUNG HEROES have been featured in the publication throughout the last decade.

To receive a free subscription to A COMMON THREAD and/or further information about concerts and retreats presented by Michael Kelly Blanchard, contact:

QUAIL MINISTRIES
121 West Avon Road
Unionville, CT 06085
(860) 673-5100

About the Author

MICHAEL KELLY BLANCHARD, who studied music at Berklee College of Music, is a native of Connecticut and lives there with his wife Greta and children Esther and Reuben.

For a third of most years, he travels the U.S.A. primarily, and Europe occasionally, giving concerts and seminars featuring his original songs and teachings.

The songwriter-storyteller has been a retreat leader and speaker at various churches, colleges, and schools throughout the country. When not touring, his time is spent home writing and overseeing Quail Ministries. He has ten albums, two full-length musical dramas, and one novel in his quiver of creations.